SUMM

A Play

HUGH LEONARD

SAMUEL   FRENCH

LONDON

NEW YORK   TORONTO   SYDNEY   HOLLYWOOD

SUMMER

First produced at the Olney Theatre, Olney, Maryland, U.S.A., in August 1974.

Subsequently produced at the Olympia Theatre, Dublin, on 7th October 1974, as part of the Dublin Theatre Festival.

First produced in the U.K. at the Palace Theatre, Watford, on 3rd May 1979, with the following cast of characters:

Richard Halvey	Rio Fanning
Trina Halvey	Brenda Fricker
Michael, their son	Mike McCabe
Stormy Loftus	James Berwick
Jan Loftus	Kate Binchy
Lou, their daughter	Bernadette Shortt
Jess White	John Rogan
Myra White	Doreen Keogh

The play directed by Stephen Hollis
Setting by Sue Blane

The action takes place on a hillside overlooking Dublin

ACT I   A Sunday in summer, 1968

ACT II   A Sunday in late summer 1974

Please note our NEW ADDRESS:
Samuel French Ltd
52 Fitzroy Street London W1P 6JR
Tel: 01 - 387 9373

SUMMER

ACT I

A hillside. An afternoon in high summer, 1968

An age-worn Celtic cross juts up at an angle near the summit. There is a suggestion of trees, and there is a wooden picnic table with flanking benches. The debris of the picnic has yet to be cleared up

The CURTAIN *rises, and the Lights come up on eight people, of whom six are married couples in early middle-age. They are: Stormy and Jan Loftus and their daughter Lou, aged seventeen; Jess and Myra White; and Richard and Trina Halvey and their son Michael, who is eighteen. To begin with, the individual families are grouped together, but not markedly so*

Everyone is quite still, as if momentarily overcome by torpor or the warmth of the sun. Stormy and Jan have brought folding stools on which they are sitting; the others are sitting or half-lying against the grassy slope. Then Myra fans an insect away from her face. Jess lights a cigarette. Lou idly teases the back of Jan's neck with a frond; Jan, eyes shut, jerks her head. Richard looks up from his Sunday Times *and squints forward. Michael, who is cradling a guitar, plays one soft chord. As if this were a signal, Stormy speaks*

Stormy One day, some right little bastard at school filled the saddlebag of my bicycle with manure off the allotment behind the sports field. I knew it would pong for a month, couldn't afford a new one. So I'm crossing the school yard with murder on me face when one of the brothers, Brother Fergal, grabs hold of me. (*He takes hold of his ear. In a Kerry accent:*) "Boy, if ye want to shtay out of trouble in dis world and Purgatory in de nexsht, take dat shtormy look off oor face." That's how I got the nickname. Stormy. I became fond of it in time. It sort of suggests . . .

Jess A dirty night.

Stormy A tempestuous nature, I was going to say. It's a great oul' standby. Fellows don't mess when your name is Stormy.

Richard (*not turning*) What does Jan call you?

Jan What do I call him? Not Stormy.

Stormy "Beloved."

Jan (*in amusement*) Ha!

Trina No, what?

Jess His name's Terence. (*To Stormy*) I didn't know you went to a Catholic school.

Stormy The stepmammy was R.C.
Richard *You* aren't?
Stormy I'm a Prod. (*Indicating Jan*) Like her.
Jan (*disliking the word*) Prod!
Stormy Certainly.

Stormy prods Jan in the ribs. She makes a bored face

Myra Jess ought to have had a nickname.
Jess Why ought I?
Stormy What's it short for—Jessica?
Myra Jesse.
Stormy That's as bad. (*To Jess*) Give us a dance.
Jess No, I'm with someone.
Myra It's not even a saint's name.
Stormy (*on his feet*) "Let's twist again,
                                    Like we did last summer,
                                    Let's twist again,
                                    Like we . . ."
Jan Terry, sit down. It's too hot.
Myra I'm baking.
Trina It's like the summers we used to have.
Lou The Twist is ancient.
Stormy Who says?
Lou It's years old. Prehistoric.
Stormy Do you hear the arrogance?
Richard (*indicating Michael*) Same with him.
Trina Stop running him down.
Richard I'm not running him . . .
Jan Louise, why don't you sit with Michael?
Lou I'm fine.
Jan They're so difficult.
Myra I hope ours are all right.
Jess Don't worry.
Myra I thought bad of going off without them. I mean, picnics are for
    children more than anyone.
Richard Yes, that's because they wreck them for grown-ups.
Myra They do not.
Richard Get off. They fall in nettles, they squabble, they bark their shins,
    slobber their food, wet their pants, get too much sun and cry to go home.
    Then they get sick in the car as a benediction.
Trina Now stop.
Richard All I'm saying is that adults, Myra included, are entitled to one
    solitary hard-earned day's outing in the year without having to
    wipe runny noses and dig latrines. (*To the men*) See? Now I'm
    heartless.
Trina (*lightly*) Oh, we all know that.

Myra I don't *want* a day off from the children. Poor little mites, sure they're only young the . . .

Jan (*ready to avert an argument*) You have how many, Myra? Three?

Myra (*her eyes lighting up*) Four. Noreen is the eldest, she's twelve; then there's Brian and Laurence and Catherine. There were five altogether, but we gave one to Holy God.

Stormy What's that, a school?

Myra I mean, one died.

Stormy Oh. Sorry.

Michael begins to smile. Richard darts him a warning look

Myra That's what we tell the children when they ask. "Little Elizabeth has gone to live with Holy God."

Jan Yes; of course they don't understand.

Myra (*unsentimentally*) They do understand. What I mean is, it's true: she has.

Myra's matter-of-factness causes a moment of discomfort

Trina Well, I wish I had as much . . .

Stormy Yeah, well, that's it. None of us know, do we?

Trina (*on cue*) No—no, we don't.

Richard *I* do.

Trina glares at him. Myra notices

(*Affecting innocence*) Pardon?

Myra (*with affection*) I don't worry myself about Richard. He's not the worst. (*She smiles at him*)

Jan Shall we clear away? There's not much point waiting for the men to do it.

Trina Catch them!

The women go to attend to the remnants of the meal. Myra stops for a moment near Richard

Myra (*in a half-whisper*) The longest way round is the shortest way home.

Richard I wish I'd said that.

Myra sticks her tongue out at him and joins Jan and Trina. Jan is brisk, setting the pace at clearing up

Stormy I think that white wine is beginning to mull inside me. (*He holds back a belch, striking his stomach gently with his fist*)

At the same moment, Michael strums another chord. Stormy looks at him, askance. Lou giggles

Richard Pity there's a haze. We lose the view.

Stormy Yeah, I have a house going up down there.

Richard To live in?

Stormy No, I'm in the trade.

Richard Ah, yes. Doing well?

Stormy You know: fair. It'll pick up, there's a few quid in the country now. God, in my young day even the Protestants were poor. A builder gets a great satisfaction. You drive down a road, you go past a house and say: "I put that up."

Richard Good.

Jess The time I used to travel for Rosanthal's the wallpaper people, I'd get the same kind of satisfaction. I'd drive past one of Stormy's houses and say: "My wallpaper's holding that up."

Stormy You bugger.

Richard Is that how you met Jess? Business?

Stormy I bought a roll or two off him out of kindness. He's a pathetic poor devil.

Jess smiles

He knows how to keep his friends well-hidden all the same. I used to see you up in the Druid's Chair Sunday mornings. Wondered who the fellow was with his eye on me wife.

Richard Me?

Stormy And of course never a word out of Jembo here that he knew you. Oh, a cute hawk.

Richard Jess and I are old friends.

Stormy Sorry for your trouble!

Trina begins to scrape the contents of a plate on to the grass

Jan Do you mind, Trina, I brought cellophane bags for the leftovers. Louise, be useful—fetch the cellophane bags. The last thing we want is a swarm of wasps.

Myra You brought everything—even stools to sit on.

Jan (*nodding towards Stormy*) That was his idea. I felt ridiculous. What does Richard do?

Trina Books.

Jan Oh, yes?

Trina Secondhand.

Richard (*overhearing*) Collectors' items, do you mind?

Trina Well, whatever. (*She winks at Jan*)

Lou (*finding the bags*) These, do you mean?

Jan Thanks, dear.

Lou sits near the cross

Myra They're so handy. Of course you can't have them in a house with children: they'd suffocate.

Stormy Is there money in that? Books?

Richard Some. People die; their libraries are sold off.

Stormy Months since I read a book.

Richard This isn't reading, this is owning. Or often they don't like the idea of their books outliving them. They say to me: empty the shelves, scatter them; nothing goes on after I die, here it ends.

Stormy People do that?

Richard Sure.

Stormy Want to take it with them?

Richard Right.

Stormy Books, huh? Tell you something: the only thing I'd like to take with me is . . .

Richard Go on.

Jess Travellers' cheques.

Stormy I've got to dig myself one of those latrines you mentioned. Stay there: I'll tell you.

Stormy goes off.

Jess What do you think?

Richard Of him? Amiable.

Jess No, I mean . . . (*He jabs a thumb towards Jan*)

Richard What *about* her?

Jess What do you think the form is?

Richard You ought to know: they're your friends.

Jess Not that I'd lay a finger . . .

Richard How could you, when you even expect me to do your lusting for you? Do you know what you are? You're a vicarious lecher.

Jess (*prompting him*) Handsome woman, though.

Richard (*disparaging*) Good for a daydream.

Jess Come on . . .

Richard embarks on what is almost an established routine, with him as performer and Jess as delighted audience

Richard A professional Protestant. Wears black jersey dresses in the evening, no jewellery. Hasn't wept since Rajah, her horse, died. Hon. treasurer and guiding spirit of the Old Folks Happy Christmas and Euthanasia fund. Highly accomplished: gives impromptu dinners for twelve in telephone booths and has a Ph.D. in flower arrangement.

Jess Sex, sex—what about sex?

Richard You're depraved, you know that?

Jess Do you think she gives him a bit?

Richard Sure, as long as she doesn't know what he's at.

Jess (*like a schoolboy*) Heeee!

Myra (*looking around*) What?

Jess Nothing.

Stormy enters

Richard I'd as soon try to climb the north face of the Eiger. No vices; no flaws; no, thanks.

Jess (*warning him*) Watch it.
Richard (*quietly*) I know. Michael . . .

Michael looks at him

The reason you're with us is to keep Louise company. Now talk to her.
Drown her with charm.

It is an order. Michael slouches reluctantly to where Lou is sitting, near the cross

Stormy He's a fine-looking lad. Is he still at school?
Richard He starts at Trinity in the autumn. He's studying to be a deaf mute.
Jan There, all done!
Myra Aren't we great!
Jan But there doesn't seem to be a litter bin. I'd better put this stuff in the car. (*She picks up the cellophane bags, now filled, and starts up the slope*)
Michael (*having steeled himself to talk to Lou*) That Ogam writing on the cross, it's a fake, you know. Wrong part of the country.
Lou That so?
Michael And—and the markings are too fresh. It probably dates from the eighteenth . . .
Lou I'll take those, mum. (*Sotto voce*) Please.
Jan (*sotto voce*) You're being rude.

Lou takes the bags from Jan and bears them off

Richard Well, help her.
Lou (*singing back*) No, thanks!

Michael shoots an unforgiving look at Richard and walks away

Jan (*to Richard*) Were *we* like that?
Richard Were you?
Jan I hope not. But if the only reason a boy talked to me was because his father told him to, I daresay *I* might put a flea in his ear, too—yes.
Richard Stick up for your own, don't you?

Jan senses a faint antagonism beneath the joke

Jan (*looking at him*) Yes.
Stormy Well, there may not be a wedding in the family, but at least we're sure of tomorrow's lunch: it went that way.
Jan Oh, you.

Michael plays a third chord, an angrier one this time. Pause

Myra Jess, sit beside me.
Jess What for?
Myra We're married. (*Incredulously*) What for!

Jess sighs and moves down to comply

Stormy See you around sometime. (*To Richard*) I'll tell you one thing: if

Jan tried to come the hound with me in public I know the answer she'd . . .

As Jess sits beside Myra she clasps his hand in both of hers

Hey up, hang on: number five is on the mat.

Trina I'm getting a tan already. (*Holding up her arms*) Richard, look: am I?

Richard Yes.

Trina I'd take my top off if I thought nobody'd mind.

Stormy We wouldn't give you a passing glance. At our age we're all beyond that sort of thing. (*To Richard*) Aren't we?

Richard Sure.

Stormy Certainly. (*He at once whips his fists up to his eyes, training them on Trina like binoculars, and emits a slavering "Duhhh!" of idiot lust*)

Trina Sure who's to see! (*She begins to unbutton her blouse, half-shyly, half-provocatively*)

Jess begins to hum "The Stripper". Stormy goes through the motions of a strip-tease.

(*Stopping*) No, I'd better not.

Stormy ⎫
            ⎬ Awwww! ⎬ (*Speaking together*)
Jess   ⎭

Richard (*irritably*) If you're all that keen, go ahead.

Trina (*in a whisper*) Michael . . .

Richard What?

Trina (*through her teeth*) Michael!

Richard For God's sake, every year on holiday she galumphs around the kiddies' paddling pool in a bikini you couldn't bandage a sore finger with, but she won't let her eighteen-year-old son see her wearing a dirty great bra.

Trina (*embarrassed*) Shut up.

Richard It's so stupid!

Myra Underwear is different, Richard.

Richard How?

Jan It is, you know.

Richard (*glaring*) Is it!

Myra (*reasonably*) Of course there's underwear and underwear in it. I mean, if it's a modest kind of underwear, then I suppose there's no harm out in the country and in front of friends. I suppose. But in front of your children is something else.

Richard You mean they're not meant to know that their mothers are equipped with breasts. I imagine that's the first thing they would have found out.

Trina He heard every word. Now that will do.

Stormy Which reminds me: I wonder if they're open yet.

Jess squints at his watch

Jess Zero minus twenty.

Jan Terry, it's very seldom we get weather like this, and we're not burying ourselves in a pub.

Stormy I thought the lads might care to wander down for a libation.

Myra (*to Jess*) You don't want to, do you?

Jess No.

Jan (*settling back*) It's heavenly.

Lou enters carrying a book. She hesitates, then walks over to Michael

Lou The *Shell Guide to Ireland* says that that cross is genuine sixth century.

Michael I never said it wasn't.

Lou Yes, you did.

Michael I said the Ogam writing on it was fake.

Lou Well, if you want to worm out of what you said I couldn't care less.

Michael Nobody is worming . . .

Lou You distinctly . . .

Michael I said the cross is genuine, the marks are . . .

Lou I'm really not interested.

Michael All right!

Stormy (*beaming upon them*) Now that's more like it!

Lou sits and affects to be absorbed in her guide book

Trina Richard . . .

Richard Mm?

Trina Over there, that red roof—is that the Tara Castle Ballroom?

Richard Where?

Trina Down there.

Richard No, the Tara Castle is miles that way, out of sight.

Trina (*who knows where it is*) Oh. We went there once.

Jan Yes?

Trina Years ago, didn't we? (*Silence*) Not since then. Just the once. (*Silence*) Years and years ago. Only the once.

Richard Trina won a beauty contest there.

Jan (*interested*) Oh?

Trina (*feigning annoyance*) What did you have to go and mention that for?

Jan A beauty contest?

Stormy (*reappraising her*) Get away.

Trina It was so silly. I can't even remember the title they gave me.

Richard It was a mountain, wasn't it? Miss Sugar Loaf.

Trina I think it was Miss Glen-of-the-Downs, Richard.

Jan What a distinction!

Myra I remember that night.

Trina It was ludicrous. I had this dress, it showed my straps. Not quite lemon-coloured, sort of buttercup—puff sleeves and a really tame scoop —(*with comic distaste*)—you know! I mean, today I'd have gone short. There were—how many other contestants?

Richard Half-a-dozen?

Trina (*overlapping*) Twelve at least.

Richard (*smiling*) More like twenty.

Trina (*laughing*) We had to—walk up and down. Sonny Fitzgerald was there. I only got up because I thought she was sure to win.

Richard (*softly*) Oh, no.

Trina And I was just beginning with Michael at the time. I mean, it didn't show, but you feel—

Jan Yes.

Trina —anything but graceful. Eighteen years ago, nineteen-fifty. And I burst into tears, didn't I, like one of those girls on the television—Miss World, all white teeth and high heels. We were out at the back of beyond—parading like cattle, big country-men roaring at us.

Richard "More o' that! More o' that, you raving beauties, you!"

Trina So I got a cheque for ten pounds, and some county councillor put this crown on my head—fourteen carat tin!—and a cloak, green velveteen, more like someone's tablecloth.

Richard (*in a rural accent, orotund*) "And in crowning this lovely young lady as the only sort of queen a good Irishman will tolerate—a beauty queen!—I express the hope of all here present that her triumph on this St Patrick's Night will spur her on to future endeavours and yield her the height of happiness as through the world she goes."

Jan He never!

Richard removes a shoe and places it on Trina's head

Richard "I now crown you Miss Rocky Valley."

Trina It was Miss Glen-of-the . . . My hair, Richard. Glen-of-the-Downs.

Myra I have a photograph of that night. Trina looked gorgeous.

Richard (*singing*) "A pretty girl—"

Stormy (*modelling*) Bumpety-bump, bumpety-bump!

Richard "—Is like a melody—"

Stormy Hello, sailor!

Richard "—That haunts you night and day,
          Just like the strain . . ."

Trina (*coldly*) Don't jeer.

Richard Who's jeering? (*Facetiously*) He's jeering; I'm not.

Trina looks at him; his expression changes to a look of ill-temper. She gives a couldn't-care-less smile to the others

Trina He thinks I'm all dewy-eyed about it. That's the mistake he makes: he's the one who's thick, not me. I mean, a dance-hall out in the wilds—it was a panic.

Jess You had a smashing old shape on you, Trina.

Trina (*with mock anger*) Had? *Had*?

Jan Well, I'm seething with envy. I always had a figure like a hallstand.

Myra It was the children destroyed *me*, God love them.

Trina Still, it doesn't last long, does it?

Jan What?

Trina That time—then. It flew.

Richard Here we go.

Trina It's nothing to be ashamed of. I liked being young. We had fun.

Stormy You were miserable.

Trina Who was?

Jan How do *you* know?

Stormy We all were. I was; you were. "Oh God, will he ring me? Will she turn up? And if she does, will she let me?"

Jan (*good-humouredly*) Now, now.

Stormy And I did ring her, and she did turn up, and mind your own business. We were so bloody wet, strutting into a hop as if you were George Raft. (*With motions of flipping a coin and chewing gum*) "Okay, sister, let's you and me shake the torso."

Jess (*to Trina, in broad Dublin*) Are yeh dancin'?

Trina Are yeh askin'?

Stormy And let one little chrissy off a backstreet with more gums than teeth turn up her nose at you, and instead of George Raft you were Quasimodo. You *limped*. (*Pointing to Lou*) They're cruel at her age: I used think they went home and practised on the cat. (*To Trina*) And you: you take a look at that photograph she's got. I bet you you had a face like a doll: nothing in it.

Jess Nice legs, but.

Trina winks and shows her knee, vamp-like. Jess releases his hand from Myra's in turning to look

Myra Jess . . .

Jess Me hand's gone dead.

Stormy In those days I thought I knew it all.

Richard And now?

Stormy Oh, now I'm wise.

Jess I love him!

Stormy Never having two ha'pennies to rub together. Slouching around the streets so's you could end the evening on a high note: in out of the cold, eating a plate of chips. No thanks.

Richard I used think I had T.B.

Stormy That right?

Richard It was the time when everyone seemed to be dying of it. They called it "The Captain of the Men of Death".

Jess He used to go around tapping his chest. (*He demonstrates*) And he didn't know whether he ought to be listening for an echo or a muffled thud.

Richard It's true. (*He clears his throat*)

Stormy Jasus, he's still got it.

Jess We used to call him "La Traviata".

Richard You can talk. This fellow got all his teeth pulled out in one go. For the next three months—

Jess One month.

Richard —he was subject to these fainting fits. On a bus, at the pictures, anywhere. One day he and I were going into Dun Laoghaire baths. We were coming down the steps, just in sight of the girls displaying their two inches of bare midriff, and he hit the ground like a sack of turnips. When he came to, they called him a sex maniac and threw him out.

Stormy Oh, them bare midriffs.

Jess (*protesting*) I had anaemia.

Stormy When you saw a bit of skin in those days you knew what you were looking at. Now it's an optical illusion. The modern girdle has more bones in it than Dean's Grange cemetery.

Myra That puts me in mind of me mother.

Stormy Does she wear one?

Myra She's in Dean's Grange.

Stormy Oh.

Myra The house we lived in, the floorboards went rotten and we had to walk on the joists.

Jan This seems to be becoming a poverty contest.

Richard If it is, you lose.

Jan Do I?

Trina Still, we were happy.

Stormy You're happy now.

Trina smiles to herself

Prime of life, the real good times not here yet. Bellies full, cars to drive home in, and instead of poverty we've got debts—that's progress.

Jess I'm too poor to be in debt.

Jan Stop bragging.

Stormy Although I suppose the young ones think we're ancient monuments.

Richard (*to Michael*) Do you?

Stormy Like the oul' cross.

Richard Speak to us.

Michael shakes his head

Why not?

Michael You only talk about the past.

Lou What do we know about that?

Stormy See, they're ganging up on us.

Michael You can't . . . (*He stops, nervous*)

Richard Yes?

Michael (*stammering slightly*) . . . Can't expect us to work up a lather over where you've been; we have enough—worries about where we're going to. Maybe you were poor starting out; well, you aren't any more,

so neither are we—so that makes us different, right? We're climbing another hill; that's why we don't b-bleed like you do.

Stormy You don't . . .?

Michael Bleed, get . . .

Lou Soppy.

Michael Show ourselves.

Stormy (*with a hint of aggressiveness*) Maybe you should.

Michael That's not for you to say, Mr Loftus.

Stormy's face tightens. Michael is afraid of him, but goes on

It's—the way things are. Mum there cries at *Random Harvest* on the
telly. I think it's a hoot, I fall about.

Myra Ah, not at *Random Harvest*, Michael.

Stormy (*dismissing Michael*) Did anyone see *Dr Zhivago* yet? Now that's
what I call a . . .

Michael Maybe she needs simple things, happy endings. I don't, and it's
thanks to them, my parents—and I mean it: thanks. 'Cause they let me
see what b-brains I've got. So I can face it that things may not end well,
me included. I don't know what to do about it, but I *can* face it, and I
don't need to be tranquillized with old rubbish.

Pause. Myra's thoughts have drifted away. She begins to sing

Myra "I'll be with you in apple-blossom time; I'll be with you . . ."

Stormy Rubbish!

Myra breaks off and looks at him

Stormy No—him. I know that if I criticized *my* parents' tastes . . .

Michael What's so terrible about that? Why shouldn't you criticize
them? You know more than they did.

Trina (*not shocked; bored*) Michael, that will do.

Michael Same as one day we'll know more than you do. Can't be helped—
we will. (*Pause. He looks at Richard*) Well, you asked me. (*He slouches
away and sits near Lou*)

Myra has resumed her song. She finishes

Stormy That was exquisite.

Myra (*assuming he means her singing*) Thanks.

Jan He's a boy.

Stormy Making a jeer of *Random Harvest*. What about them and their
Elvis the Pelvis?

Myra I loved Greer Garson.

Trina Poor James Dean is dead these thirteen years. Would you credit it?
Nineteen-fifty-five. I was mad for him. I still love him.

Richard Necrophilia.

Stormy (*absently, still smarting*) She was good, too.

Jan and Richard look at each other and burst out laughing

What's up? (*Scowling at Michael*) Did he upset you?
Jan (*incoherently*) No . . .
Stormy What's the joke, then?

Richard points at him, unable to talk

Trina What?
Jess I didn't hear it.
Stormy (*getting annoyed*) If it's so funny, let's in on it.

Jan explodes into another paroxysm. Richard sits on the bank, laughing painfully

Ah, this is a cod. I'm asking you what's so . . .

Jan waves him away

Am I the joke, is that it?

Myra begins to giggle

What are *you* laughing at?
Myra (*losing control*) I don't know.

There is a sudden alarming shriek of falsetto laughter from Jess

Stormy Jasus, now what?
Jess (*pointing at Richard*) Him.
Stormy What about him?
Trina Tell us.
Jess What he's . . .
Stormy What he's what?
Jess (*shrilly*) What he's . . . sitting in!

Richard leaps up, feeling the seat of his trousers. Now it is Stormy's turn to laugh: great humourless gusts which are punctuated by Jess's Stan Laurel-like shrieks

Trina (*in revulsion*) Oh, Richard.

Then she, too, joins in the laughter. Jess staggers over to one of the folding stools and sits. It collapses, pitching him to the ground. The laughter escalates. Michael buries his head in his arms, while Lou faces away, her shoulders shaking

Jess (*kicking his feet in the air*) Stop . . . oh, stop.
Richard It's too much.
Trina (*wiping her eyes*) Oh, my God.
Stormy (*holding his chest*) No—no—no—no-o-o-OH!

It is, finally, a cry of pain. His face registers alarm. He sinks to his knees, gasping for breath, his eyes bulging

Richard (*still laughing*) Look, he . . . (*He realizes that Stormy is ill*)

Jan Terry? (*She goes to him*)
Myra What is it?

Jess emits another hoot of laughter

 Jess!
Jan It's all right. (*To Stormy*) Don't panic, darling. Take a deep breath.
He gorges himself—all that French bread. You aren't going to die, but
if you will eat like a pig this is what you must expect.
Richard I think it's his heart.
Jan Fat chance. His trouble is six inches further down. (*To Stormy*) Get
some air in: gulp. Did you bring your tablets?

Stormy shakes his head, agonizedly trying to belch

Myra Has anyone any baking-powder?

Trina looks into her handbag, then stares at Myra, who shrugs helplessly

Jess He gave that potato salad a terrible death.
Jan And the piccalilli, *and* the cheese. (*Wiping Stormy's forehead*) You
won't learn, will you? As greedy as a child—which you aren't any
longer.
Stormy (*belching*) Excuse me. (*In relief*) Oh, God.
Richard How is it now?
Stormy I'm doing the breast-stroke in me own sweat. I'm okay.
Jan (*to Richard*) And you talk about taking children on a picnic!
Myra (*to Jess*) See? We could have brought them.
Stormy Humblest apologies. But yous don't get rid of me that easy. I've
got a ticker like a donkey engine.
Jan Donkey is right.
Lou (*shaken*) I thought he was . . .
Michael He's fine. In middle-age the digestive system collapses, that's all.
Stormy (*looking at Michael*) Lou, your dad will be around to give you a
silver-wedding present. Now what we all need is a stretch of the legs.
Jan He's mad.
Stormy Through the woods to the top of the hill, down the grassy lane,
turn right at the road and . . .
Jan And look where we are. A pub! How did that get there?
Stormy I need a soda water, Jan.
Trina I'm sure.
Richard I don't mind, if you're up to it.
Jess I'm on.
Myra (*privately*) No.
Jan At least let him rest for a minute. (*To Stormy*) Yes, you will. Now
please.

*Stormy makes a martyred face. They subside. Michael strums a chord. The
Light changes so that the couples are separately key-lit by spots. The lighting*

of the unoccupied areas becomes muted. There is an effect of individual isolation

Stormy I feel like a wet dish-rag.

Jan He looks awful.

Myra (*to Jess*) I thought I was going to have to say an act of contrition into his ear. Except he's a Protestant. What do you do in that case?

Jess Say it into his left ear.

Trina All that laughing has made my eye-black run. Ah, look at me: I'm a fright to the world. (*She begins repairing the damage*)

Richard (*looking at Stormy*) Poor fellow: he's more frightened than ill. God, if he knew I'd been out with his wife he'd really have a heart attack.

Richard and Jan look at each other briefly. Jess surreptitiously counts his money

Jess I'll need a quid for petrol for tomorrow's calls. (*He tucks a pound note into his sock*) If they don't drink shorts I'm not too bad. Wait now: Trina's on vodka, Jan is gin and tonic. So if Richard sticks to beer and Stormy takes soda water . . . Only he won't; he'll want brandy to recuperate.

Jan I'm not going to see him again. I sat in that pub trembling in case one of our friends walked in. Not that they'd ever tell: it'd spoil their fun. The sense of power.

Jess (*retrieving the pound note*) I can get the petrol on tick, and if I have a good breakfast I can skip lunch. Yea.

Stormy What if it *had* been the old ticker? I'd hate to pop off on a summer's day: all that invigorating sunshine gone to waste. The depth of winter, now, when the blood is thin and you can't lay concrete: that's different. I mean, for preference. Rain or shine, poor old Jan'd take it very hard.

Jan I'm insane. A married woman going on forty, having her head turned like a schoolgirl because a man is interested. Well, no harm done, but not again: no, thank you.

Myra It's a sin. It's a sin to spend money in public houses with children's mouths to be fed and clothed. How can we expect God and His holy mother to help us if we won't help ourselves?

Trina (*to her mirror*) You'll do. You'll more than do. Men still look at you, do you know that? They squint at you sideways, think you don't notice. In the pub Sunday mornings, eyes like spiders. They strip you to your skin, but wouldn't give you an honest-to-God up and down look if it killed them. Too soon after Mass! But I see them. (*She laughs knowingly and puts her mirror away*) Now I don't mind where we go. As long as the day lasts. I'm sick and tired of days ending. (*Instantly bored, she begins to hum "A Pretty Girl is Like a Melody"*)

Myra (*through the humming*) I wish I was at home now tucking them in, and Jess telling them a story.

Jess Once upon a time there was this princess, and she met a prince. And they were as keen as mustard. And one day she gave him a kiss, and he tasted smashin', so he did. So she ate him.

Richard She sat in that pub, so bloody poised. Fine bones, posh accent— end of inventory. Thin as a lath and cold as January. The Queen chatting up a comedian: "And when one falls arse over tip, does it hurt?" I bet it would be like kissing a cobweb. No, forget it.

Stormy Back page of the *Irish Times*. "The offices of T. E. Loftus and Co. will be closed today as a mark of respect to our late managing director, Mr Terence-bracket-Stormy-bracket-Loftus, dearly beloved husband of Jan and father of Louise Hilary. Will those who think of him today, a little prayer to Jesus say." (*He wipes his eyes*)

Jan Discreet, though: no-one would guess. Too damn discreet: he's been needling me all day. That wasn't pretending.

Jess You've got to look prosperous. If I could afford a decent suit I could get new customers . . .

Richard I'll try to get her on her own later on and cancel Tuesday.

Jess But until I get new customers I can't afford a decent suit. Every penny goes to the kids. One of these days the girls will be the best-dressed nuns in the convent.

Myra I always liked Richard. He has a good heart, he'll turn to God in his own time. (*She looks at him*)

Trina She wouldn't have that dawny look on her face if she had to live with him. All he's good for is finding fault. He thinks I'm some kind of joke just because I try to be a credit to him.

Jan Tomorrow evening, the Victoriana society; coffee morning on Wednesday; ways-and-means committee Thursday. And damn, the Gleasons for dinner on Friday.

Richard (*watching Jan*) Still, she's thinking about me.

Jan I'll serve them a paella.

Trina He says *I'm* vain, when that aftershave he has on would knock out a horse. *He's* not eighteen years old any more either.

Stormy That young pup upset me, saying all we ever talk about is what's past and done with. Is it! Give me ten years and all them fields and woods down there will be gardens. Then there'll be a view worth looking at from here.

Trina (*looking at Myra*) Maybe he'd like to be married to *her*. A house like a slum because all she bothers to keep clean in it is her soul. Look at Jess, the heels out of his socks.

Jess catches her eye and winks at her

(*Brightly*) Hi.

Jan Louise isn't sticking to her diet. That child's so overweight, and she doesn't seem to care.

Jess I can see up Trina's leg. I'd love to get off my mark with a fast bit of stuff. Just the once, to think back on. I keep meaning to, only I never get round to it. Maybe when I get the new suit.

The guitar strikes a chord. The Lights come up as before

Stormy Well, are we right?
Jan Are *you* all right?
Stormy (*mock-lecherously*) Will I prove it?
Jan I think I feed him too much red meat.
Stormy Very active woman, the wife. She was going to leave me once, but she couldn't fit it into her week.
Richard Here we go, then. Lead on.

They all rise and start to march off

Jess Quick march. Hup! Hup!
Myra Jess, not so fast.
Trina My heel is caught—wait!
Stormy Stragglers will be shot out of hand. Step it out—lift them! (*To Michael and Louise*) The pair of you, come on.

The group marches off, talking as they go

Michael and Lou watch them as they walk away

Michael Do you want to go with them?
Lou No. You can.
Michael (*shaking his head*) I don't think your dad fancies me.
Lou That's odd.
Michael Yeah.
Lou He's usually a *bad* judge of character.
Michael (*laconically*) Oh, devastating.
Lou Another Einstein!
Michael Who is?
Lou Saying you know more than they do.
Michael I said I will, one day. Not now. I don't know anything yet.
Lou You said . . .
Michael What?
Lou Those marks.
Michael Ogam.
Lou That they were fake.
Michael They are.
Lou Einstein!
Michael Sure, and I can tell you that Dublin is there—(*pointing out front*) —and Wicklow is that way (*to his right*). And Robert Kennedy was killed three weeks ago, and the atomic weight of mercury is two hundred point sixty-one, and in case you want to propose to me, this year is a leap year. But that's not knowing: I took someone's word for it. I haven't found out one thing for myself yet.
Lou All right: what colour's my hair?
Michael Fairish.
Lou (*triumphantly*) See? You know that my hair is . . .

Michael No, I don't. Someone told me that colour is called fairish.

Lou Oh, get shredded.

Michael (*professorially*) Now of course you will argue that every so-called fact must have a given hypothesis—

Lou I'm not *going* to argue. Go to Trinity. Persecute *them*.

Michael I will. At least there'll be people there I can talk to, because at home it's useless. It's the modern generation of parents. They don't listen, they're out till all hours, they rush around in cars. If they see a Porsche that's doing ninety, they have to pass it, but they won't pass a pub that's standing perfectly still. I dunno, they're too young for their years, they're missing their adulthood.

Lou Let them.

Michael (*pointing*) I mean, look at them now.

Lou Where?

Michael There, are you blind? They're out of sight.

Lou turns away wearily

We sit here calmly, conserve energy. They go rushing over precipices like lemmings.

Lou Because they're older than we are. They can't be sure they can rush until they try.

Michael I asked my dad a question yesterday—just so's he wouldn't feel out of things. I said: "Do you believe man is by nature a monogamous animal?" Did I get the courtesy of an answer? He looked at me as if I was a red infiltrator and he was John Wayne.

Lou I may go to Trinity this year.

Michael Waste of time.

Lou Thank you.

Michael For girls it is. Any girl. You do four years' hard slog, take your degree, then go and get married. It's like saving up to buy a Masarati when all you want is the ashtray.

Lou You're nasty.

Michael I'm a realist, what's wrong with that? Time enough to be a romantic when I'm middle-aged.

Lou And for your information, I don't intend to get married.

Michael That so?

Lou Not for diamonds.

Michael It's just as well.

Lou Boys bore me. What do you mean, it's just as well?

Michael (*backing down*) Nothing.

Lou I suppose you mean I'm not likely to be asked.

Michael No! All sorts get ... (*He stops, aware that he has made matters worse*)

Lou (*unrelenting*) Do they?

Michael I mean, when you see some of the gargoyles who ... (*He stops again*)

Lou A girl doesn't have to be as thin as a rake, you know.

Michael (*conciliatory*) Sure.

Lou Or dye her hair, or have eye-lashes you could whisk eggs with. Pointy bosoms, that's what men are supposed to be mad for, isn't it?

Michael Are there pointy ones?

Lou Not half.

Michael (*politely*) That's worth knowing.

Lou Fiona Mulligan, she's in fifth year, hers are like daggers.

Michael Get away.

Lou You'd cut yourself.

Michael Deary me.

Lou I really do pity that sort of girl. All the time rushed off their feet, never get a minute's peace and quiet. And the sort of creepy-crawlies they always go out with—ugh.

Michael I know, yes.

Lou And of course they get married years too soon and live in the same house till doomsday. I'd hate that. No, when I look at them I'm honestly and truly glad I'm the way I am.

Michael (*feigning innocence*) What way is that?

She gives him a knowing and bitter smile

I've seen worse than you. Real clock-stoppers. (*As her smile congeals*) What?

Lou (*shaking her head*) I'm just so thrilled I came out today.

Michael (*uneasily*) So what are you going to do?

Lou Go for a walk.

Michael After Trinity.

Lou (*with unfeigned intensity*) I'll tell you one thing: I won't stay here, not in this hole. I'll get a working scholarship and go abroad. Places like Israel and America and New Guinea. Northern Labrador, maybe.

Michael What's in Northern Labrador?

Lou Do you know—well, I forgot; you don't know anything, do you?— that some Eskimo women kill their second-born on account of in the Arctic there are no vegetable foods and the mother has to nurse her first child until it's three years old? Helping those people, that would be wonderful.

Michael They're real primitive, right?

Lou Some are.

Michael Yeah, you see photographs of them. All in furs. And the Eskimo women . . .

Lou Poor things.

Michael They're *really* fat. (*Meaning it kindly*) You'll look thin when you go there.

Lou looks at him in dismay. As tears start to come, he begins talking from sheer panic

You've got your life all cut and dried. I don't. Give me a mystery tour any day. With me it's like . . . Did you ever play rugby. (*As she stares at him*) No.

Her weeping takes on a new fury

I do. And you daren't relax. You can't even blink an eye, 'cause when the ball comes you've got to be there. That's me: I wait for it. Life. Honest, I get so tensed up, I shake. This is it. You catch; don't drop it; hold on to it. Except—it's not just one single big event that happens, it's a million little things, all different, and if one gets past you they all will. No, come to think of it, it's not like rugby. Rugby is just one ball; life is a lot of balls.

He nods to himself, wisely. Lou's shoulders begin to shake

Are you laughing or crying?
Lou I don't know.

He puts his hand on her breast. As she looks at him, stupefied, he grins, says "Ow!" as if he had cut his fingers, and puts his hand to his mouth

What are you doing?
Michael Daggers.
Lou What? You're bonkers.
Michael First time I ever did that.
Lou And the last.
Michael See what I mean? There's another little thing I caught hold of.

She inspects her bosom, wondering if this is to be taken literally

(*Happily*) It must be the weather. On a day like this there's nothing you can't do. (*Shouting*) Not—one—damn—thing!
Lou Except whisper.
Michael There isn't.
Lou Let's walk down.
Michael Think of you in Labrador eating dog-meat sandwiches and doing your D.B. degree in an igloo.
Lou What's D.B.?
Michael Doctor of Blubber.
Lou I'll get further than you will.
Michael Think so? I can take up rally-driving, stamp-collecting, five-card stud or read Nietzsche.
Lou (*derisively*) You?
Michael I can work for my dad in the bookshop or dig sewers or push a pen or pull teeth. Anything! I can marry a nice bright sharp little bird, or the sort if you looked in one of her ears you could see out the other; or the neurotic destructive kind that goes in for black net stockings, or . . . (*He stops*)
Lou Or what?
Michael (*almost slavering*) Black stockings . . . oh, God.

Lou (*contemptuously*) I'm going to catch up with them.
Michael One thing's sure: when it begins I'll be ready.
Lou When it begins?
Michael Living. Race you to the pub.
Lou It's too far.
Michael On your mark, get set . . .
Lou That's not fair. Wait.
Michael Go! (*He starts to exit*)
Lou (*calling after him*) I don't know the way. I'll get lost.

Michael and Lou exit

The Lights change to indicate a lapse of hours: the sun's rays are now oblique

Richard and Jan appear over the crest. Jan stays on the summit

Jan We shouldn't have left them so far behind.
Richard Where are you going?
Jan (*as if he should know better*) To where they can see at least one of us. (*Looking off*) He's sitting down.
Richard Who?
Jan Jess. (*Waving*) Coo-ee! (*To Richard*) Is he tight?
Richard Pissed.
Jan Yes?
Richard Three pints and he's anybody's.
Jan How many do *you* need?
Richard Pints or women?
Jan I've heard stories.
Richard Where?
Jan The village.
Richard About me?
Jan And women.
Richard Anybody I know?
Jan Joan Armitage.
Richard *Who?*
Jan They say you and she . . .
Richard Joan Armitage?
Jan You do it awfully well.
Richard What?
Jan Innocence. Years of practice, I expect. (*Looking off*) They're heaving him up.
Richard I've never even been . . .
Jan No, he's down again. Poor Jess.
Richard Not once.
Jan My dear man, I couldn't care less.
Richard Nor could I.
Jan (*a blank smile*) Oh, good. The children seem to be squabbling again.

What a waste of fine weather.

Richard The village is a gossip factory, you know.

Jan (*in the voice she uses for small-talk*) Yes, it's the most flourishing of our cottage industries. I wish they wouldn't.

Richard Gossip?

Jan Squabble.

Richard (*coldly*) I think I'll lend them a hand with Jess.

Jan You said in the pub you wanted to talk to me in private. What about?

Richard Yes, I did.

Jan Well?

Richard About Tuesday . . .

Jan I think we should scrub Tuesday.

Richard So do I.

Jan It's mutual, then? How super.

Richard Yes, jolly hockey-sticks.

Jan (*with a gesture*) So off you go to the rescue.

Richard (*hesitating*) Purely out of interest . . .

Jan What?

Richard Why are *you* cancelling Tuesday?

Jan Purely out of *lack* of interest.

Richard is offended. He opens his mouth to speak; instead he makes what he hopes is an ironic bow and starts off

Face it: we didn't exactly hit it off.

Richard We were too close to home.

Jan Oh, come on.

Richard (*stubbornly*) If we had met nearer to town . . .

Jan You must be touched.

Richard How?

Jan Because of all women, you pick on me. I'm thirty-nine—as my husband keeps reminding me, in five years' time I'll be forty. I have a home to worry about, and a daughter who's a recluse at seventeen. I do so much committee work, there aren't enough days in the week, and I promise you, you'd find that cross sexier than I am. And still you want me to skulk around bars and restaurants and sit mooning with you in a car after the pubs close. No, you go and find some nice unhappy lady who needs that sort of thing. Hm?

Richard I thought I'd found her.

Jan (*smiling*) Oh, no.

Richard Foiled again.

Jan Yes, you are.

Richard I just cannot resist a posh accent.

Jan Is *that* the attraction?

Richard Blue-bloods. Women who ooze refinement.

Jan Me?

Richard Unflappable.

Jan And that excites you?

Richard It's what my son would call a turn-on. As if I'd come across a rare first edition.

Jan You mean something to curl up in bed with?

Richard Too risky. In bed I stick to the cheap paperbacks.

Jan At least this explains Joan Armitage.

Richard Does it?

Jan She's awfully grand.

Richard Yes, if she were a lesbian she'd be a thorough gentleman.

Jan Another rejection? Oh, poor man. (*Looking off*) Good, they're coming. Now there's someone who adores you.

Richard Trina?

Jan Wives don't count. Myra.

Richard She thinks I'm a nice man.

Jan You and she meet secretly.

Richard When?

Jan (*tapping her head*) In here.

Richard It would have to be. The nearest Myra ever comes to making a date with someone is when she says "We'll meet in heaven."

Jan Purely out of interest . . .

Richard What?

Jan Why did *you* want to cancel Tuesday?

Richard grins

Richard Purely out of . . .

Jan (*as a challenge*) You dare!

Richard Your reason is as good as any. What was it you said? Skulking around bars. Childish.

Jan (*in her small-talk voice*) Have you skulked much?

Richard Beginner's stuff—nursery slopes kind of thing. I mean, my skulk never got as far as the slalom class.

Jan Slalom? I thought that was a Jewish good-bye.

Richard Only if you fall into a crevasse.

She giggles; we see the girl underneath

It just isn't worth it. Mind you, if it was a question of a great volcanic all-devouring passion . . .

Jan You'd run like hell.

Richard You reckon?

Jan A man who takes jolly good care to chase after the kind of woman who won't have him? You'd run ten miles.

Stormy and Trina enter

In the distance a church bell is heard. It rings for about a minute

Stormy *I* couldn't run ten feet. I'm bunched.

Richard (*wondering if they have overheard*) You got here!

Stormy Thanks for giving us a hand with Jess the Mess.
Richard I'd no idea he was that bad. Where is he?

Stormy gestures off

Trina His legs went all rubbery.
Stormy Yeah, he wasn't so much drunk as vulcanized. The fresh air does it every time. I always say, if you go into a pub, stay in it for the sake of sobriety.
Trina (*looking off*) Now *Myra* is on the ground. No, she's only praying; it's the Angelus.
Jan (*looking at her watch*) Six o'clock?
Richard Your wife and I have decided to break off our affair.
Stormy That a fact?

Jan, caught off guard, attempts to play up

Jan Yes, before it starts.
Stormy Pity. There goes our mixed foursome.

Trina slides her arm through Stormy's. While the gesture is meant to seem mock-amorous, the afternoon's drinking has made her mildly lustful

Trina Sure we can play a singles.
Richard Oh, do.
Trina (*warmly*) Can't we, Blowy?
Stormy Stormy.
Jan (*sotto voce*) Is she . . .
Richard No, just tipsy.
Trina You don't mind us at all. We're having an intimate conversation. (*To Stormy, hazily*) What about?
Stormy Indoor toilets.
Trina (*squeezing his arm*) Yeah.

Trina looks at Stormy with intensity. He either does not notice her unwavering stare or pretends not to

Stormy I was saying, I foresee the day when every home will have a minimum of three.
Trina That right?
Stormy The ivy-covered privy in the yard may have been good enough for our parents. These days people want a plurality of toilets to make up for their years of deprivation. Have you me?
Trina I have you.
Stormy An astute man would corner the market in toilet bowls now.
Jan Dear God.
Stormy Or better still, invest in vitreous china. (*Including Richard*) Sanitation is a fact of life. If I had capital I'd sink everything I had in toilets.
Trina No flies on you.
Stormy (*to Richard*) It's worth a flutter.

Trina Talk to *me*. (*As Richard looks at her*) Is something up with you?
Richard No, love.
Trina (*antagonistic*) Love!
Richard (*to Jan*) Have you a busy week ahead?
Trina (*in a mutter, mimicking*) Have you a busy week ahead?
Jan Only frantic.
Richard Committee work?
Jan There's no end to it.
Trina I never got my tan. (*Lifting her skirt*) Did I, Windy?
Stormy (*squinting skywards*) You won't get one now.
Trina I think maybe I have a little bit of one.
Stormy Sun is too low.
Trina Would you say I have a bit of one?
Stormy (*absently*) What?
Richard (*snarling*) For Chrissakes, Windy, tell her she has a bit of one!
Jan Now, now.
Stormy Yeah, all she asked was . . .
Trina 'S all right. I don't mind him.
Jan Hear, hear.
Trina (*very grandly*) I don't give a shite.
Stormy That's the good girl.

Jan holds up a finger, forbidding Richard to speak

(*Chattily*) The haze is lifting. It's not often in this country our summer happens on a Sunday, what? (*To Trina*) I say it's great weather for laying a cement path, as long as you damp it well.
Trina Not even allowed to flirt.
Stormy 'Cause if you don't, it'll crack, as sure as shootin'.
Trina Like living with Hitler.
Stormy (*gently*) Ah, shush.
Trina A squeeze of the hand to let you know you're not dead—no harm in that. A bit of messing on a summer's day. Yeah? 'S nice. Different if it wasn't open and above board.
Richard No one is . . .
Trina Old jealous-boots. You'd think I went in for hole-and-corner carry-ings-on like—like some.
Stormy Now you're talking, Trina. Down in the town—Jasus, it's like the Roman empire: they're all at it. You'd think it was Judgement Day and the archangel had stood up and said: "Good news, ladies and gentlemen —adultery doesn't count."
Trina He's never done belittling me.
Richard Belittling?
Stormy Compared to them we're saintly.
Richard (*to Jan*) Show her a newspaper and all she reads is "Mutt and Jeff" and "The Wizard of Id".
Jan Oh, stop it.

Stormy Playing with fire. What gets into people?

Jess enters, Myra by his side. He is boisterous and affectionate, waving his arms

Jess (*singing*) "Those—were—the days, my friend,
We thought they'd never end . . ."
Stormy Jess, me oul' flower!
Jan (*to Myra*) Is he all right?
Myra I laddered a stocking saying the Angelus.
Jess The angel of the Lord declared unto Myra. No better woman!
Richard Are you well?
Jess I'm in great form. Treen, come here to me. (*He embraces her clumsily*)
Trina He was at me again.
Jess *I'd* like to be at you, Treen—true as God.
Myra I love him when he jokes.
Trina Always when I'm enjoying myself.
Jan (*to Richard*) Yes?
Jess Ah, life's too short. Enjoy it like I do.
Trina (*bad-temperedly*) Jess, leave off!

She breaks away from him, causing him to stagger. He grins fixedly to hide his bruised feelings. She smoothes her dress and hair

Jess I like to annoy her.
Myra Richard wouldn't upset Trina.
Trina (*bridling*) You're the expert?
Stormy She was saying about the goings-on down in the town. Ordinary lads—your Joe Soap that maybe grew up same as you did, in a house where he had to walk on the joists. Every second one of them at it like a fiddler's elbow.
Myra At what?
Jess Ridin', what else.
Myra No.
Stormy Look. (*On his fingers*) George Canaan going with Tim Corboy's wife. Dave Giffney and Finnuala-butter-wouldn't-bloody-melt-McArdle. Des Luby who's in church furnishings, at it as if there was no tomorrow with Chad Whelan's missus . . .
Jan Stop gossiping.
Stormy And what about your one with the teeth and the gold-embossed accent—Joan Armitage? If it moves and if it's male, she's under it.

Richard stares at Stormy. Jan begins to laugh. Jess busily takes notes on the back of a cigarette packet

You'd want to have leprosy with complications before that one'd say no to you. (*To Jan*) You may laugh, but it'd take an IBM machine to keep up with them.
Myra (*serenely*) One day you'll get sense, boy.

Stormy Think so?

Jess How do you spell Armit——

Stormy What?

Jess (*as they look at him*) Nothing.

Myra It's play-acting, and sure what harm? God love them, they think they're great. It's like the children out on the road playing cowboys, with the badges on them and the toy guns.

Stormy (*sourly*) Yeah—bang, bang.

Myra Dressing up to be what they're not—all excited. And even if it was true, what you say they're doing, aren't we all children of Eve? They'll get sense.

Stormy (*a great arm-flapping gesture of resignation*) I give up.

Richard There's a man called Joe Pettifer . . .

Stormy He's a dipso.

Richard He goes into Hogan's and stays clear of his wife. Her pub is the Mariner's. Pauline. She has a three-star rating in the local graffiti. Most nights at closing time some kind man gives her a lift home by way of a back road or a building site. God alone knows why she does it, maybe her looks went . . .

Jan Does he know?

Richard He weeps, he slobbers. He confides in total strangers, half of whom gallop straight down to the Mariner's. I used to think, if I were that man I'd walk into the sea. The kids have left home, he has nothing. One day Trina and I went to a wedding . . .

Michael and Lou enter

Michael Hi.

Lou We came back by the . . .

Richard holds up a hand: a salutation and to get attention

Richard There was dancing afterwards. Ragtime. And there was Joe Pettifer playing a bloody banjo.

Trina (*remembering*) Him? Was that . . .

Richard Sweat pouring off him. And he was good: they cheered. Happiest man in the room . . . (*He pauses*)

Michael strums a chord

Stormy Can you play that?

Michael Wish I could. It's ornamental.

Trina We ought all to go to a dance, the six of us. That's my idea of an evening. (*Indicating Richard*) He's hopeless. But Jess always asks me up.

Jess (*loftily*) Not any more.

Trina makes a face at the others as if to say "What's biting him?"

Myra We'll have to make a move soon. I want to get him to bed before the children come home from their granny's.

Jess Bed?

Myra I'll tell them he has a toothache.

Jess I've no teeth.

Myra Or a cold. We don't want them to see you.

Jess Hide their glasses. (*To the others*) Four children—sixteen eyes between them. Our youngest looks like Ben Turpin.

Myra Who?

Jan Myra, why don't I take our car, and Terry can drive you and Jess home in yours?

Jess I can drive; no better man.

Myra Do you hear him? He'd give St Christopher a nervous breakdown.

Stormy We'll stop by for a jar at our place.

Myra No—straight home.

Richard Same here. Early start in the morning.

Trina (*speaking from the side of her mouth*) I want to see their house.

Richard I want to see ours.

Richard crosses to Jess and speaks to him, a hand on his shoulder. Jess shakes his head stubbornly

Stormy (*during the above*) Five past six—the day's only started.

Jan Don't oblige them. (*She folds up a stool*)

Stormy One drink won't kill you.

Trina It'd kill *him* to be sociable. (*She starts to clear the picnic things*)

Richard Make it up with her.

Jess I'm not dirt.

Richard I know.

Jess She made little of me.

Richard She's squiffed.

Myra Jess . . .

Jess (*peering at Trina*) She's never!

Richard She's flying.

Myra We're going home.

Richard So be big.

Jess (*solemnly*) Them that can hold their gargle make allowances for them that can't. Trina . . .

Richard Attaboy.

Jess leads him over to Trina and puts an arm about the shoulders of each

Jess No hard feelings.

Trina (*friendly, not knowing what he refers to*) Not a bit of it.

Jess You're a livin' doll.

Trina Am I? Aw!

Jess And you offended me, but I forgive you.

Trina Good.

Jess 'Cause Richard has apprised me of your condition.

Trina's smile fades

Richard Thanks, Jess!

Jess (*hugging him*) Me old comrade. Since we were that high.

Richard Right.

Jess The time we robbed old Threadgold's orchard. (*Indicating Jan*) And her da chased us.

Richard Whose da?

Jess Her da. Mick Goggins—the rozzer, the policeman. That lived in the Cottages.

Richard (*to Jan*) You're one of the Gogginses?

Jan I was.

Richard From the Cottages?

Jan What of it?

Richard Where'd you get that accent?

Jan (*proudly*) Hard work!

Richard Well, I'm . . .

Jess (*plucking at his sleeve*) Hey, hey . . .

Jan You are, rather, aren't you? (*She skips away from him, humming "The Rain in Spain"*)

Jess I say, I had a smashing day.

Stormy We all had.

Myra (*to Jess*) No speechifying, now.

Jess And I haven't a tosser. Do you know what that louser I work for did last week? Put me on straight commission. Times, he says to me, are hard. A man that can buy his wife a shagging Volvo for a run-around, telling me that times are hard! Catch him getting snotty letters from the nuns for school fees.

Myra (*smiling*) Oh, you're in a bad way.

Jess I am. I could pass through the eye of a needle with me arms extended. And you know what? . . . bugger it! I have me mates, and we still have the long evenings.

Myra Home now. Where's your jacket?

Stormy I see it. (*He moves to fetch it*)

Jess We'll pull the divil be the tail somehow.

Myra (*tidying his hair*) *You* have it pulled out of him. If you lowered less drink into you . . .

Stormy fumbles with Jess's jacket

Jess Yeah, yeah.

Myra The sun splitting the heavens, and us stuck in a pub.

Jess Blame me! He drags us in and I get the . . . (*He stops, looking at Stormy*) What are you doing in my pocket?

Stormy Nothing.

Jess Gimme that.

Stormy I wasn't in your . . .

Jess (*snatching the jacket*) You need watching, mate.

Myra Nobody was next or near your . . .

Jess I had a few jars, but I'm not ossified. (*He pulls a dirty handkerchief from the jacket pocket*) Here—here, all I've got.
Richard Easy . . .
Jess Do you want it? Have it.

Stormy, fists clenched, is holding his temper in check

Trina Ah, Jess.
Jess It's not safe to go out any more. Take it. Here. (*He tosses the handkerchief at Stormy's feet and turns his back on him*)
Stormy You pick that up. (*Dangerously*) Jess . . .
Jan That's quite enough.
Stormy No one is going to call me a . . .
Jan The word wasn't said—don't you say it.
Stormy He accused . . .
Jan Today is not going to end with a row.
Stormy (*pointing*) That . . .
Jan (*furiously*) Will you shut up!

Jan glares Stormy into silence, then bends, picks up the handkerchief and gives it to Myra

Myra It needs ironing.
Jan Myra and Jess have to go home now. So do we.
Stormy He can drive himself, then.
Jess You watch me.
Myra No . . .
Jess Downhill all the way, do it in neutral.
Stormy (*with a mirthless laugh*) Jasus.
Jan (*to Myra*) Don't mature men make your toes curl?
Myra (*earnestly*) Oh, yeah. 'Bye, Richard, we had a great time.
Richard Safe home, Myra.
Trina 'Bye.
Myra (*to Jan*) It was the drink talking, don't mind him. (*To Louise and Michael*) God bless, now.
Lou   ⎤ 'Bye.   ⎤
Michael ⎬ Yeah, see you. ⎬ (*Speaking together*)
Stormy ⎦ Mind yourself. ⎦
Jess (*to Richard*) It was a . . .
Richard A what?
Jess A day you could frame. Give us a buzz. (*To Stormy*) All the best, so.

Stormy looks away

Benny the Dip is not talking to me.

Stormy, still angry, finds himself trying not to laugh. He keeps his back to Jess

Aw, he's crying.

Jan (*mock-angrily, pointing off*) Jess, go home.
Myra (*waiting for him*) Jess . . .
Jess Have you got me hanky.
Myra Yes!
Jess Another robbery thwarted!

Stormy swings around

> (*Singing*) "Those were the days, my friend,
> > We thought they'd never end . . ."

Jess and Myra go out of sight

Stormy Messer.
Richard How much did you put in his pocket?
Stormy (*sheepishly*) Didn't get the chance. (*He unclenches his fist to reveal two crumpled pound notes*)
Jan Is *that* what the . . .
Stormy Do a fellow a favour!
Trina Nice man.
Stormy Now I'm Benny the Dip.
Richard Serves you right.
Trina It's more than you'd do.
Jan Terry, don't let him drive, go after him.

Stormy is about to protest

> Yes, you will. Louise and I will follow you.

Stormy (*to Richard*) You'll notice I know better than to argue. I'm glad we got together. We ought to make a thing of it.

Jan pushes Stormy

Jan Yes, come and have dinner.
Richard Love to.
Stormy (*to Jan*) You fix it.
Jan (*pushing him*) Yes—now hurry.
Stormy I'm saving his life, and you know the thanks I'll get? By tomorrow he'll have it all around the town that I'm queer for dirty handkerchiefs.

Stormy waves to them and goes

Trina He's gorgeous.
Jan Yes?
Trina So considerate.
Jan When the humour takes him. I like this spot; we ought to come back, it's unspoiled. (*To Lou and Michael*) Have a nice day, you two?
Lou Super.
Michael Yeah.
Jan Their eloquence is positively Shakespearian. Damn.
Trina What?

Jan My considerate husband has gone off with the car keys. Louise, would you . . .?

Lou runs off. We hear her calling "Dad . . . the keys!"

Jan goes to the summit and watches her

Richard (*to Trina*) You have a good day?

She shrugs and starts clearing up again

No?

Trina You've been at me since we got up this morning. I can't do nothing right anymore.

Richard Anything right.

Trina Christ almighty.

Richard (*martyred*) Sorry . . .

Trina I have to take every word out of my mouth and look at it.

Richard Don't start a . . .

Trina Then telling Jess I was drunk.

Richard You were mauling Stormy.

Trina (*raising her voice*) Mauling?

Jan probably hears the following, but gives no sign

Richard Shh . . .

Trina A bit of affection.

Richard Shout, why don't you?

Trina More than I get from you.

Richard Yes, all right.

Trina (*lowering her voice*) "Act your age. Read this book. Don't wear that dress. Take up something, join something, do something."

Jan (*looking off*) She's got the keys. Good girl!

Trina You'd like me to rot, that's what'd please you, isn't it?

Richard Of course it would.

Trina To be like them, puffing themselves up with their sales-of-work and their meetings, making a noise to cod themselves that they're not dead and done for. Not me, no damn fear.

Lou enters with the keys

Jan Bless you, you're a jewel. (*To the others*) Shall we stroll down together?

Richard Let's. (*To Trina, a peace offering*) We could have dinner out this evening, if you like. At the Castle.

Trina I'm not mad keen.

Richard It would save you from cooking.

Trina No, I don't want to.

Jan Yes, about dinner—when can you come to us?

Richard You say.

Jan Tuesday? No, wait. (*Looking at him*) No, I'm meeting a girl friend on

Tuesday, in town. So that's out.

Richard (*after a pause*) I see.

Jan Of course I could cancel it.

Richard Don't. I have to be somewhere on Tuesday as well. A late night.

Jan Mine won't be. Home by eleven. (*Including Trina*) We're having people over on Friday. Come then.

Trina That'd be great.

Jan Eight for eight-thirty. Well, then . . .!

Trina, Jan and Richard start up the slope

Trina Richard . . .

Jan Come along, young 'uns.

Trina I can't go into the Castle like this. I'm not dressed.

Richard We'll go home first.

Trina I can wear my long black.

Richard Sure.

Trina With the see-through top.

Richard What else!

Trina is childishly pleased. She takes Richard's arm as they start off

Jan (*favouring Trina*) I want to pick your brains. The Borough Council wants to take down a Victorian lamp-post in Harbour Road. It's of historical value, so of course we're going to stop them. Question is: how? Now, if we got up a petition, could I rope you in to . . .

Jan, Richard and Trina exit

The attitude of Michael and Lou during the following is of affectionate parents

Lou Do you think they enjoyed themselves?

Michael I'd say it did them good.

Lou It makes a change.

Michael Mine had a row. (*He collects up the stools*)

Lou Oh. (*In the sense of "What a shame!"*)

Michael Nothing drastic.

Lou That's 'cause they got too much sun.

Michael Yeah?

Lou It makes them bilious.

Michael How?

Lou Too much of it.

Michael Queer. I mean, it's the smallest star known to man. It's big, but its density is only one-point-four-one times that of water. You wouldn't think it could upset them, would you?

Michael and Lou go

Immediately, the stage fills with blinding light, followed by a Black-out, as—

the CURTAIN *falls*

ACT II

The same. Six years later, August, 1974

The Celtic cross has gone; in its place is a notice board. The trees—if any were visible previously—have been chopped down. We can see part of either a crane or a mechanical digger. The picnic area is substantially as it was, but we sense that it is now hemmed in, encroached on, and soon it will disappear. The sunlight has a hardness which suggests that the day is chilly A young woman walks on and takes off her sunglasses to read the notice board. It takes us a moment to recognize Lou, who is now slim and self-possessed. After a moment Stormy and Jan appear. He has put on weight and wears an expensive mohair suit. Jan's clothes echo the rise in his fortunes, but now there are lines of stress in her face that were not there previously. Stormy carries a picnic hamper, a rug and an expensive cassette player. He stares at the view

Stormy This is not the place.

Jan Why isn't it?

Stormy Where's the fields?

Jan (*looking front*) Someone's been busy.

Stormy And I say we took a wrong turn.

Jan You're so pig-headed . . .

Lou There used to be a Celtic cross.

Stormy Good girl. (*To Jan, crowing*) The cross, where's the . . .

Lou (*reading*) "St. Eanna's Cross, which stood on this spot, has been removed to the National Museum of Ireland."

Stormy It's been what? (*He reads the notice*)

Jan You see? I said this was the . . .

Stormy (*heavily*) Full marks.

Jan But of course you'd argue black was white.

Stormy Christ, I said I was wrong, you don't have to make a meal of it. (*He looks, blinking, at the view*) There's nothing left.

Lou It's awful.

Stormy Those are Bellavista Houses, I'd know them a mile off. How did the buggers get permission?

Lou For what?

Stormy To build. Down there used to be country.

Lou Not now.

Stormy Even this place is ear-marked—the cross is gone: national monument.

Jan Who cares?

Stormy God almighty, that's a million quid's worth of land. Someone got his palm well-greased.

Jan You missed the bus, then, didn't you?

Stormy You never saw me grease a palm.

Jan No?

Stormy When did I?

Jan The houses at Churchtown.

Stormy That was a favour. I didn't pay.

Jan (*drily*) Oh.

Stormy Back-scratching is one thing. Paying money is corruption.

Lou Two of them have swimming pools.

Stormy Snob jobs.

Jan A bit out of your class.

Stormy (*coldly*) Get off my back.

Jan Gladly.

Stormy You know damn all. (*Pointing*) It's them—your thirty thousand quid hilltop homes—that land the independent builder into the bankruptcy courts. And before you turn your nose up at Corporation houses, they're what paid for the clothes on your back and the bits of Georgian silver you're so mad about. No-one is asking you to live in one.

Lou (*lightly*) Bicker, bicker.

Stormy Not that it would be a come-down for you after the Cottages.

Jan Thank you.

Stormy Tit for tat.

Jan Yes, well done.

Stormy That house there isn't finished yet. I'm going down for a squint inside it.

Jan Go.

Lou (*looking off*) Here's someone.

Jan Who?

Lou The Halveys, I think: there's three of them.

Stormy (*turning back*) Ah—Richard: good.

Jan Lick his boots, why don't you?

Stormy How?

Jan Do you have to be at their beck and call? We've waited for them; let them wait for us. (*Starting off*) Well, are we going to look at that house or aren't we?

Stormy There's a wasp in you today.

Jan I'm not going to be trampled on.

Stormy No-one is . . .

Jan goes off

Lou I'll hang on.

Stormy Yeah, tell them. And mind the stuff,

Stormy follows Jan

(*Off*) What the hell's up with you?

Lou looks up at the sun and hugs her arms as if chilled

Michael appears. His hair is much longer now; he is dressed as befits a trend-conscious young man of leisure; a suit of suede denims, perhaps. He carries a picnic hamper

Lou Hello.
Michael 'Afternoon. (*He fails to recognize her, and looks about him*)
Lou Lovely day.
Michael Not bad. Cold for August.
Lou I'm . . .
Michael (*catching sight of Stormy and Jan and calls off*) Mr Loftus! (*Waving*) Hello!

Michael exits with the hamper

Lou is immensely pleased with herself. She whirls around, crowing with delight

Richard and Trina appear. There is no obvious change in him, but Trina has lost her previous petulance. Her clothes—perhaps an attractive trouser-suit—are no longer too young for her. Richard carries two stools, Trina a freezer bag, cushion and rug

Richard Look who's here—Louise!
Lou Hi!
Trina Doesn't she look fab?
Richard Blooming.
Lou I *hate* that word.
Richard (*kissing her*) Here—prerogative of age.
Trina (*laughing*) Any excuse!
Lou Trina looks younger.
Trina Sure—than your granny.
Richard No-one else here?
Lou They went to look at one of the houses. Isn't it frightful?
Richard (*now noticing*) Yes, it is.
Lou Ugh!
Richard And not one of them Stormy's. He missed the bus.
Lou That's what Mum said.
Richard I know. (*After a pause*) Did she?
Trina Richard, look at all the lovely houses!
Richard (*with a wink at Lou*) Breathtaking.
Trina (*taking his arm*) Well, they are!
Richard (*to Lou*) You home for long?
Lou Just the week-end.
Richard So how are things in foreign parts?
Lou Oh, Cork hasn't changed.
Richard Fine city.
Trina We haven't seen you since . . .
Lou The wedding.
Richard Was it?

Trina And how is . . . (*She forgets the name*)
Lou Pearse?
Trina Pearse!
Lou He's fine, sends his love.
Trina He's not with you?
Lou He did want to come. But if he doesn't work every week-end this month we can't take a holiday next month.
Trina Shame.
Lou And of course there's a fat chance of one next year, with a newborn yelling it's head off. (*Giggling*) I must tell you . . .
Trina What?
Lou Michael . . .
Richard Where is he?
Lou He walked straight past me.
Trina No!
Lou Said "Good afternoon", looked through me, and—(*She breaks off*)

> *Michael enters, with the hamper. He makes an elaborate gesture of penitence*

Richard You're a right nit.
Michael It's been five years, do you mind?
Lou Six.
Michael You've seen her since then.
Richard When did the penny drop?
Michael *They* told me. (*To Lou*) Sorry.
Lou I'm thrilled.
Michael Yes?

Lou smiles, catlike

Trina Do you remember that day, Michael?
Michael When?
Trina Here. (*To Richard*) Hadn't we a great time?
Richard It was pleasant . . .
Trina (*fondly*) Head like a sieve. All of us as happy as Larry. Except poor Jess got this . . . (*Touching her chest*) upset. Bilious, like.
Lou It wasn't Jess, Trina, it was . . .
Trina The fright he gave us. I don't forget one detail. (*To Richard*) You had to drive him home.
Richard I never . . .
Trina Yes, you did. The good old days.
Richard (*to Lou*) Don't argue.
Michael You live in Cork?
Trina Happy as Larry!
Lou Crosshaven. My husband is with the refinery at Whitegate.
Michael That's—in Northern Labrador?
Lou You brat, you remember!
Richard What's in Labrador?

Michael She isn't.

Lou I was seventeen. (*Primly*) If everyone went where they'd set their hearts on going when they were fat and foolish . . .

Michael Then Ireland would be full of Eskimos.

Lou makes a face at him

Trina Michael is a . . . (*The word escapes her*)

Richard Bio . . .

Trina Bio-chemist!

Lou Are you? From know-nothing to know-all.

Trina (*laughing*) Oh . . .!

Michael The Cork air is sharp.

Richard (*to Lou*) Do you like Cork?

Lou I wish I could get home oftener. That way you don't notice the changes. The bad ones. Mummy doesn't look well.

Trina How?

Lou She looks—tired. Do you not think so?

Trina The thing is, Louise, we . . .

Richard We haven't seen them in—

Trina Haven't laid eyes on them—

Richard —in a month.

Trina More. Nearly two.

Richard Haven't had time.

Trina (*about to argue*) Now . . .

Richard (*stronger*) Haven't.

Trina (*not antagonistic*) You could have made time. You have time for Jess.

Richard Jess hasn't been . . .

Trina (*to Lou*) He doesn't go to the Druid's any more on a Sunday. Says he's tired of it, wants a change. The times Jan and Stormy ask us out: no, he has work to do.

Lou I'm sure he has.

Michael You *can* go off people. *I* do.

Richard I went off no-one. If I didn't have your mother's accounts to keep as well as my own . . .

Trina That excuse!

Richard All I'm . . .

Trina (*amiably*) He blames me. Who was it bully-ragged me into finding an interest?

Richard I'm not disputing . . .

Trina Calling me a vegetable. Yes, you did. Whose idea was "Treenager"?

Lou Was what?

Trina That's the name of it. The shop. "Treen" for Trina—and then sort of like "teenager". You come in tomorrow, Louise—I have a full-length for you in Italian loose-knit will have the Corkmen's eyes out on sticks. (*To Richard, soberly*) No, Stormy is fond of you, and you're not a good friend to him.

Richard I'll make amends.

Trina Do.

Richard Give him a French kiss.

Trina Shut your mouth.

Michael Funny kind of French kiss that'll be.

Trina Oh, like father, like . . . Louise, don't laugh at them.

Lou I'm not. I was picturing myself in an Italian loose-knit a few months from now.

Trina Won't it keep! You aren't going to be expecting twelve months out of every year, are you, like . . . Myra, hello!

Myra enters, followed by Jess, who—instead of a picnic hamper—carries a papier-mâché attaché case. She has happily embraced middle-age: there are streaks of grey in her hair and her figure has thickened. Jess is a bit older, a bit scruffier: his old ebullient self is subdued; his mind seems to be focused on something within himself

Myra (*catching her breath*) Whoo! We got here.

Richard Here she comes—let the good times roll!

Myra (*looking around*) Jess!

Jess I'm here. (*To the others*) Hi.

Myra Hello—hello. (*With instant emotion*) Louise . . .!

Lou How are you, Myra?

Myra Such great news!

Lou Oh, you heard?

Myra I can't come over it. Jess—Jess, look at her.

Lou It doesn't show?

Myra (*comforting*) Now have patience. You'll be out like a house in no time.

Trina Won't that be worth waiting for!

Richard nudges her; she slumps against him. Lou keeps a straight face

Myra When's it due?

Lou Early Feb.

Myra Winter—mind its chest.

Lou I will.

Myra Have you morning sickness?

Trina My-ra!

Myra What?

Trina Don't talk shop.

Lou And how's Jess?

Jess Smashin'.

Michael You look great.

Richard Leaps and bounds.

Myra He's to mind himself.

Jess I am.

Myra No catching colds.

Jess It's August.

Myra Summer is treacherous. And no worrying.

Jess (*to Richard*) I've had a clean bill since last . . .

Myra It can come back.

Richard No.

Myra It can, if he worries.

Jess Then stop worrying me. (*To Richard, forcing a grin*) Bloody stupid thing to get at my age.

Richard Who's "La Traviata" now?

Jess (*not rising to the joke*) Yeah.

Richard Have you noticed the new scenery?

Jess (*not looking*) Nice.

Myra (*mainly to Lou*) We all had to go for X-rays. I couldn't credit it, I mean, you do your best and then you have a thing like that in the family.

Richard Myra, come out of the dark ages.

Myra When I heard that word . . .!

Richard You'll regard this as heresy, but a spot on the lung is now considered respectable. You carry on as if it was V.D. he had.

Jess No such bloody luck.

Michael goes over to Myra, who is looking sullenly at Richard

Michael Myra—it's a bacillus, right?

Myra I suppose so.

Michael A bacterium called the tubercle bacillus.

Myra (*stubbornly*) He didn't get it in our house.

Michael gives up

Jess (*suddenly*) I heard a riddle.

Richard Tell us.

Jess It's a good one.

Lou is admiring a medal which Myra wears around her neck on a chain

Lou Myra, that's gorgeous.

Myra It's the Blessed Virgin.

Lou Beautiful.

Myra I've had it these many years. Louise, if you're that taken with it . . .

Jess I said, I heard a riddle.

Myra We're listening, pet.

Jess You won't guess it.

Lou (*impatiently*) Oh, Jess!

Jess What do you call an uncircumcized Jewish child?

A moment's pause

Trina A girl?

Jess looks at her, his face thunderous

   (*Innocently*) Is it?

Richard Hey, not bad. Where'd you hear that?
Jess A priest told me.
Myra (*now laughing*) Oh, it's very funny.
Lou (*pointing off*) Hey, I know that face.
Trina Whose?

Stormy and Jan enter

Stormy The meeting will now come to order.
Trina He's arrived!
Stormy (*to Trina*) How are you, luscious?
Myra Hello, Jan.
Jan Myra, don't you look nice. Hello, Michael.
Michael Hi.
Jan (*to Richard, with a too-bright smile*) Hello.
Richard How are you?
Jan And Jess!
Stormy And fresh and well he's looking. (*He kneels before Jess. Singing*)
        "Your tiny hand is frozen,
            Let me warm it into li-ife . . ."
Jess (*retrieving his hand*) Bugger off.
Stormy (*to Richard*) And where the hell have you been?
Richard Around.
Stormy Well, we're black out with you. (*To Jan*) Aren't we?
Jan Completely.
Richard No reprieve?
Jan None.
Stormy Once herself puts the knife in . . .!
Trina Blame him.
Jan We do. (*Ignoring Richard*) How's the boutique?
Trina Mmm—wait till you see our Autumn range. We're showing it next
    month in Jury's.
Jan Aren't you grand!
Trina Not at all: the only people not exhibiting are the pawnshops. (*In
    a stage whisper*) But I'm doing better than he is.
Jan (*politely*) Yes?
Stormy (*to Richard*) Are you raging?
Richard Livid.
Myra Sure isn't it in the family?
Trina Oh, no. (*As a catch phrase*) What's his is mine and what's mine's
    my own.
Richard Don't think she doesn't mean it.
Jan Good for her. (*Turning to Myra*) Are the children well?
Myra Grand, the whole six of them. And I have news.
Trina Myra, not another one!
Myra (*waving this aside*) Ah, wait. Noreen is getting married after Christ-
    mas.

Jan *Is* she?

Myra She'll be the first to leave us. Well, we did our best. We made sacrifices for them, and they'll do the same for theirs.

Jess And so on and so on.

Myra Please God.

Jess Like a recurring decimal.

Myra What?

Jess So where's the pay-off?

Myra He's very morose.

Stormy He's hungry. We're famished.

Richard We can't eat here.

Trina Why can't we?

Richard Look at it. By the time we're finished someone will have built a house around us.

Michael It's a bit late to go ploughing off into Wicklow.

Stormy (*to Jan*) What do you say?

Jan Well, if it means we've got to drag the stuff all the way back to the cars . . .

Myra Jess has to take things easy.

Lou And the sun's going in.

Stormy Out-voted.

Richard (*with a gesture of surrender*) All right, we'll sit here and count garden gnomes.

Stormy Girls—get cracking. I'm that hungry I could eat a baby's bum through a cane chair.

Jan (*smiling uncertainly at Richard*) Sorry.

Richard shrugs off-handedly. Jan tries to keep her voice light

Blame me. I thought: what a good idea if we all came back here, seeing as Louise and Michael are with us. I mean, we've put it off for so long.

Richard Well, we're here now.

Trina Will we pool everything or stick to our own stuff? Jan?

Jan (*looking at Richard*) Yes.

Trina Which?

Jan (*coming to*) Let's share.

Michael Can I help?

Trina Just stay clear.

Stormy (*motioning Michael to join the men*) Young lad . . .

Myra I'm awful: all I brought was sandwiches.

Trina Don't worry.

Myra I didn't cut the crusts off.

The women unpack the food on the table. The business of serving it in individual helpings will take several minutes. There is chicken, ham, potato salad, French bread, cheese, pickles, etc. The men move well away from this activity. Stormy puts a finger to his lips and produces a nest of metal cups and a hip-flask. He pours and passes the cups around

Stormy To whet the old appetite.

Richard Splendid.

Stormy Have a taste.

Jess What is it?

Stormy Pewter.

Jess No, I mean the . . .

Stormy Anniversary present, cost a mint. (*To Michael, serving him*) Try that.

Michael Cheers.

Stormy (*warning him*) Shhh . . .

Jess Good stuff.

Richard Need we ask how's business?

Stormy Making a quid. You?

Richard Surviving.

Stormy These days if you're cute you go in for quantity. I have a new estate under way at Pine Valley. Four units to the acre.

Richard Bit on the small size.

Stormy No, no. Compact.

Richard Sure.

Stormy It's the modern concept: space elimination.

Myra Trina, look what she brought. Strawberries.

Trina Ooh!

The Men Oooooh!

Trina Pack of jeers.

Jan There's no cream to go with them. Terry's on a cholesterol-free diet.

Myra Jan, I envy you.

Jan The strawberries?

Myra Going to be a granny.

Jan looks at Myra coldly

Lou Don't bet on it.

Myra While I have to wait a whole long year.

Jan A year?

Myra Till Noreen is nine months married.

Trina Ah God, Myra, she's not a greyhound.

Myra How?

Trina I mean, at a wedding you're supposed to have a prayer-book, **not a** stop-watch and a starting gun.

Myra (*beaming*) You're just an old jealous-boots because Jan and me **are** going to be grannies.

Jan Myra, must you use that word?

Myra What word?

Jan While we're handling food.

Lou Oh, mum.

Jan Well, I'm sorry—it's a horrid word, it belongs in a geriatrics ward. It's maudlin, it wears a cameo brooch and black taffeta. It . . .

Stormy switches on the cassette player: a Beatles number: "When I'm Sixty-Four"

Do we need that noise?

Stormy It's what we brought it for.

Jan It's your toy, *you* brought it.

Stormy (*to the men*) Great power, what?

Jan I said, turn it down.

Stormy (*doing so*) 'Scuse me for breathing.

Richard They get moody.

Stormy Yeah-yeah. (*To Jess*) Refill?

Jess shakes his head

Come on, you look as if one more clean shirt would do you.

Jess looks at him as if struck

I'm coddin'.

Jess Sure you are. (*He turns away*)

Stormy Hey, take a joke.

Richard What's up with you?

Stormy (*nudging Jess*) Have a jar.

Richard Is it what Myra said?

Stormy When?

Richard She was going on at him a bit about . . . (*He touches his chest*)

Stormy Oh. Well, with respect to Myra, Jess, she knows as much about T.B. as my arse knows about snipe-shooting.

Richard You had a mild dose. You're over it.

Jess I know. I know I am.

Richard Cured.

Jess Yes.

Richard Then what's wrong?

Jess I'm going to die.

Jess tries to grin at them. The muscles of his face twitch; tears come into his eyes. Stormy switches off the cassette player

Sorry.

Stormy Where'd you get that for a yarn?

Jess (*rubbing his eyes*) Hang on . . . (*He takes out his handkerchief, grubby as previously*)

Richard nudges Michael, who moves away

No-one told me—I just . . . 'Scuse me. (*He wipes his nose and sniffs loudly*)

Richard Take your time.

Myra (*to Jess*) Have you a cold?

Jess No.

Stormy If no-one told you, how do you . . .

Jess I can't—stay alive.
Stormy Balls.
Richard Are you ill?
Jess (*indifferently*) Dunno.
Richard Then . . .
Jess Couple of years ago, Myra and I flew over to stay with her sister in Bradford. Bit of a holiday. Myra thought flying was a great gas—five miles nearer to God. I was scarified, spent the whole time trying to keep the damn thing airborne. (*He clutches an imaginary arm-rest*)
Richard Me too.
Jess Yeah. Well, I can't any more, I can't keep it in the air, I've let go. Yous know me: am I a begrudger? See fellas getting on in the world: best of luck. As long as there was the couple of jars, me mates, something nice tomorrow. And old Myra the same: happy with the kids and the boy friend.
Stormy Who?

Jess points at the sky

Jess But when I had to go into the san, that was it. I said: Jesus, can't I win once in my life? Not a war, not a battle—is one lousy skirmish too much to ask? At night I'd look out at the fir trees and wonder if they'd planted evergreens so's we wouldn't know when the summer was gone. I lay there and I thought: why couldn't it be that pair for a change? You and you. Only it never rains on them that has umbrellas. You know what's dangerous? Laugh at a man when he hits you. He takes your money: tell a joke; he takes your job: sing a song. And if you won't cry, sooner or later he'll bloody well kill you.
Stormy Is that all that ails you? You sap, you.
Jess (*trying to sound matter-of-fact*) You can't win, let go.
Stormy Bullshit. (*He offers cigarettes*)
Jess Gave them up.
Richard (*refusing also*) Jess, you'll bury the lot of us.

Jess shakes his head violently. Tears well up again

Stormy You'd have something to whine about if you were Martin Hewitt. Playing golf on Friday, funeral tomorrow. And him only forty . . .

Richard shoots him a warning look

No, no—nearer sixty. Still, it's young.

Myra talks to Lou

Trina Grub's up!
Richard (*to Jess*) Watch it.
Jess I'm okay.
Trina Don't stir, we'll wait on yous hand and foot.

Stormy Proper order.
Jan Oh, no, we won't. Let them stretch themselves.
Trina Come and get it, so.
Richard (*to Jess*) Come on.
Jess (*rubbing his eyes*) Wait.

Myra still talks to Lou, who is anxious to change the subject

Lou Myra, I really couldn't tell you whether he is or not. You'd better ask him.
Myra How can I ask . . .

Lou goes to Michael with a wine bottle and a corkscrew

Lou Open this for me, would you?
Jan Myra?
Myra All I said was, was Pearse excited about the baby?
Stormy Pearse? (*Angrily*) That little . . .
Jan (*warning him, not severely*) Terry . . .
Myra What is it?
Jan It's nothing . . . shhh.
Stormy When I get hold of him——
Jan Myra, that's Jess's. (*Serving Stormy*) Now, diddums, this in ums right hand this in ums left hand.
Richard (*singing*) "And the rowlocks between ums knees . . ." (*He nudges Jess*)
Jess (*joining in*) "And we'll all sing together,
                    For as long as we damn well——"
Trina This is not a singing pub. (*Handing Richard a plate of food*) Richard . . .
Richard (*taking his plate*) Looks fantastic.
Stormy Where's me garlic bread?
Jan No bread for you. Nor cheese, nor hard-boiled eggs.
Stormy Aw, Jasus.

Myra comes down to Jess with his food

Myra We saved the sandwiches. You can have them for your lunch tomorrow and—(*she stares at him*)—
Jess What?
Myra —and Tuesday.
Jess We were laughing that hard. (*Raising his voice*) I was telling them, in the san I always knew when the children were praying for me. The bed used to levitate.
Myra (*reproachfully*) Jess.
Jess (*guffawing*) Spiritual streptomycin.
Stormy Oh, a bad bugger.
Trina Now dive in, make a start.
Myra Trina, wait.

Trina What for?

Myra Grace.

Jess Lovely girl, you'll like her.

Myra "Bless us, oh Lord, and these Thy gifts which we are about to receive from Thy bounty, through Christ our Lord, Amen."

Trina Amen.

There is a general movement as they each pick a place to sit

Lou (*to Michael*) You pour, I'll serve.

Michael Nothing wrong?

Lou No.

Richard This fresh air—I'm ravenous.

Trina moves to sit with Richard, but Jan gets there first

Jan (*to Richard*) May I sit with you?

Stormy It's a mixty, is it?

Jess (*sotto voce, to Myra*) I want a word with Stormy.

Myra Well, have it.

Jess Private—it's business.

Myra Mind your suit.

Trina Here, Myra—old maids' corner!

Myra and Trina sit together. Jess sits beside Stormy. Michael and Lou distribute the wine

Stormy (*to Jess*) Look, starvation diet. Hey—swap.

Jess What?

Stormy Gimme your plate. Now keep between me and her.

Trina How is it?

Stormy Smashing.

Jan I made the garlic bread.

Richard Delicious.

Jan Try tasting it.

Lou serves Stormy with wine

Stormy Attagirl.

Lou moves to Jess

Lou Jess . . .

Jess Thanks, Lou.

Lou (*as American air hostess*) You're entirely welcome, sir.

Lou and Michael sit together. Richard samples the garlic bread

Jan Yes?

Richard Mm!

A silence as everybody eats. Stormy wolfs his food

Jess You won't broadcast what I told you?
Stormy When? God, no.
Richard (*calling across*) How are you doing?

Stormy gives him a glimpse of the garlic bread

Trust you!
Lou Mum, it's super.
Michael Better than super.
Jess (*to Stormy*) Meaning to ask you . . .
Stormy Ask.
Jess Noreen's wedding . . .
Stormy We'll be there.
Jess No, the thing is . . .
Stormy Get's another bit of bread. Discreetly.

Jess goes to the table for the bread

Jan Does Michael still live at home?
Richard Yes. Says there's no point in paying money for a flat since he
doesn't have a girl friend.
Jan (*as a joke, with no undercurrent*) Well, what else are flats for?
Richard Indeed!
Jan Doesn't have a girl friend?
Richard Hasn't time.

Jess returns with the bread

Jan At his age?
Richard So how have you been? Keeping well?
Jan (*still smiling*) No.

Richard's face darkens with ill-temper

If you don't want to be told, you shouldn't ask.
Richard My mistake.
Jan Just—don't offer me your politeness. (*Eating, in her party voice*) Mm—
it's not bad.
Myra (*to Richard*) You're getting it!
Richard Who is?
Myra You. From Trina.
Trina Don't mind him. So his lordship waltzes in, calm as a millpond, to
say he's used the money my poor mother left me to take a lease on the
old baby-linen shop. In my name!
Myra Not a word to you?
Trina Oh, a back-stabber.
Myra (*to Richard*) Are your ears red?
Trina I said to him: "Me, run a boutique? I couldn't sell ice-lollies in
Purgatory."
Jess (*to Stormy*) While they can't hear us . . .

Stormy Have manners, me mouth's full. Sit forward.

Trina I wasn't in the place a week before I found out the women in this town would wear flour sacks if you stuck an Italian label on them. Now I wouldn't be parted from that shop.

Myra You may thank Richard.

Trina Mm . . . (*To Richard*) Thanks.

Stormy (*to Richard*) Hey, you missed it at the Druid's.

Richard Did I?

Stormy Monica Riordan threw a tumbler of vodka at Noreen Cooney. Said to her: "That's for sending my husband home to me crying his eyes out." Uproar.

Richard Nasty.

Stormy No, it was the August Bank Holiday. People feel they ought to do something special.

Jan Like throwing vodka?

Stormy Better than sitting at home.

Jan (*to Stormy*) Eat your food. (*To Richard*) What if I threw this in *your* face?

Richard looks at Jan

No. (*She drinks*)

Richard Don't get fraught.

Jan Fraught? Do you know—(*she gets her voice under control and smiles for the benefit of the others*)—how miserable I've been? Or care?

Richard Not here.

Jan All right, where? (*With self-anger*) I swore I wasn't going to behave badly. That's another of your accomplishments. I had pride at one time.

Richard You'll drop us both in it.

Jan Have I . . . (*She stops*)

Richard What?

Jan A successor yet?

Richard Will you stop?

Jan (*looking around*) They're gossiping. Have I?

Richard No.

Jan Trina looks happy. (*As this gets no reaction*) I hate seeming a bore, but after six years it would be nice to be given a reason.

Richard You got one.

Jan That makes sense.

Richard (*about to move*) Excuse me.

Jan (*gripping his arm*) Don't go. I'll be as good as gold . . .

Myra looks at them, curious. Richard raises his glass

Myra All the best.

Jan Please . . .?

Jess (*to Stormy*) I need three hundred quid.

Stormy You what?

Jess For the wedding. Excuse abruptness, I hate borrowing. It's a big day for a girl. Your Louise—now she was fantastic: all them yards of lace and stuff. Thing is, you don't get many oohs and aahs ploughing up to the altar in a pink going-away suit. It's okay for some, but people like us—we're too poor to get married on the cheap.

Stormy Three hundred.

Jess We saved a bit—Myra saved it. Then I got sick and it melted. I'm driving an untaxed car.

Stormy That's bad.

Jess I did me sums. I can pay you back half of it by April, guaranteed, and the other half this time next . . .

Stormy How can you pay me back if you're going to die?

Jess stares at him.

(*Crowing*) Gave the game away, didn't you? You're a fake, a fraud. Own up.

Jess Yeah.

Stormy Next time get up early in the day, what? So how come you didn't ask him first? (*Nodding towards Richard*) Your buttie.

Jess He's not doing too well.

Stormy Trina'd give it to him. She is.

Jess He couldn't ask her.

Stormy Why couldn't he?

Jess (*tight-lipped*) Because.

Stormy (*letting it drop*) Three hundred. Jess, you're a friend, so I'll do you a favour.

Jess Thanks. I'm . . .

Stormy Not a tosser.

Jess half smiles at him, not believing

Why? Because borrowing never helped anyone. They get out of the woods, they sit on their hunkers, it happens again. Jess, I've been through that mill. You're in a mess, you pull yourself out, and that's what builds character.

Jess It's not character I'm asking for.

Stormy You're an improvident sod. I lose sleep over you, you know that? I say: where's he going to finish up? A wife, six kids, and it's all come-day, go-day, God-send-Sunday. Man, shift your backside. Do like I do—move!

Jess I need it.

Stormy Jess, for your own good, no. You want to harm a man, lend him money.

Jess Then harm me.

Stormy laughs aloud

Trina There they go: dirty jokes.

Stormy He's a riot. Drop of the hard stuff—good for you. (*He pours Jess a drink from the flask*)

Lou (*to Michael*) What's her name?

Michael Shhh—Catherine.

Lou Don't they know about her? Why not?

Michael She's married.

Lou Oh?

Michael Separated, of course.

Lou Well, sure.

Michael If the old man knew, he'd hit the roof.

Lou Your dad?

Michael Don't let him fool you. He's one of the great do-your-own-sexual-thing advocates of nineteen-forty.

Lou What would your mother say?

Michael Cry. Then sell her something.

Lou Do you live with her?

Michael In this town? No way.

Lou If you're fond of her . . .

Michael She's fantastic, but if you live with someone you're not going to be very big socially, are you? The only friends you make are in the same boat as yourself, and who wants them? People tell you they're broad-minded, but just you try getting put up for a golf club.

Lou (*incredulously*) Do you want to?

Michael Not now; but I may do. Catherine won't be around forever; I mean, I'm bound to meet a nice girl, the kind you get married to. Why bugger it up? Then there's the job.

Lou Bio-chemistry?

Michael Play it by the rules and at forty-five you're top dog. I do research.

Lou (*impressed*) Wow. Is it cancer research?

Michael As important as. I work for Blizzard.

Lou What's Blizzard?

Michael Oh, come on, get with it. Detergents.

Lou Washing powder?

Michael Among other products. What's wrong with that?

Lou It's not exactly Louis Pasteur, is it?

Michael No, it's not. But then Pasteur never had stock bonuses or a company car. How much missionary work have you done lately? (*He helps himself to food*)

Trina Jan . . .

Jan Hello.

Trina Myra was telling me . . .

Jan What?

Myra Ronan, our second youngest was nearly run over at the People's Park. They ought to put a zebra crossing there, Jan, they ought to.

Trina And they drive like it was Brand's Hatch.

Myra We thought if your committee got on to the Borough Council . . .

Jan I gave up that nonsense years ago. But talk to Molly Bolger: she'll
get them after it like wolves. (*To Richard, quietly*) I gave up all that sort
of thing to make time for us. You were jealous then—even of that poor
old Victorian lamp-post I wanted to save. You pounced on every
minute I had as if it was yours and you'd lost it. Once I even invented
a committee, for the pleasure of watching you wheedle and nag and
bully me into resigning from it.

Richard True?

Jan But times change. Now you tell me to find an interest, get out more. I
burned all those bridges, and you expect me to unburn them. I don't
have Louise any more—like her mother she has a fondness for men who
don't want her.

Richard Louise?

Jan There's no-one. And I miss you.

Lou (*to Michael*) You'd get on with Pearse, he's a jazz buff, too. That's
where I met him—a Dave Brubeck concert.

Michael I was at that!

Lou Inside a week I was six pounds lighter, and that was the end of the
Eskimos.

Michael Are you sorry?

Lou Not a bit—thanks to him.

Michael Who—Superman?

Lou For your information, I'm not starry-eyed. I mean, he's fantastic, but
he has his faults.

Michael (*feigning shock*) Pearse?

Lou One or two. Like—(*lightly*)—he's a panic—he said to me, "My dear
Louise, would you kindly inform me how we are to get to the pub and
the yacht club with a newborn to look after?" He's twenty-six years old
and his life's gone: I stole it. "This is your child, you have it, you stay
at home with it—I won't."

Michael He said that?

Lou I mean being married—it's giving up things—like they did. He'll
grow up, give him time. Only now there's either long silences or he's off
out with his friends. (*Her voice falters*) I *suppose* it's with his friends.

Michael Now come on!

Lou Yeah. Last—when was it?—Wednesday, he crept in with the dawn.
I was waiting up. He looked at me as if I was a thief in the house. So I
came home.

Michael Not for good?

Lou Get sense, boy, what would I stay here for? No, we'll make it up.
No bother!

Michael (*looking at Jan and Stormy*) Do they know?

Lou Part of it. It was different in their day; with them if it's not black it's
white. Still, I'm not nice. Poor old Pearse, down there all on his own-
some. (*She giggles*)

Richard (*to Jan*) We were a public joke. The whole town knew about us.

Jan They knew within a month.

Richard And sooner or later . . .

Jan Here it comes.

Richard (*indicating Stormy*) He would have found out.

Jan I disagree.

Richard And Trina.

Jan If we'd been honest——

Richard Sure.

Jan —we'd have told them.

Richard And gone away.

Jan Others have done it.

Richard I can't.

Jan No, you're special!

Richard I don't know where "away" is. And I find . . . (*He stops*)

Jan Go on.

Richard I find it a bit late in the day and more than a bit stupid to swap one loneliness for a worse one.

Pause. Jan puts a hand over her mouth. He looks towards the others in alarm

Jan You should know by now I don't cry. I get sick sometimes; I don't cry.

Stormy (*to Jess*) You're in the sulks.

Jess I'm not.

Stormy You're mad at me.

Jess I'm brooding.

Stormy Over what?

Jess Money. If I don't get it somewhere Noreen can go to the altar in her pelt and the St Vincent de Paul can do the catering.

Stormy You'll get it.

Jess Not unless I print it.

Stormy You'd persecute a saint, you know that? (*Taking out a cheque book*) And I'm worse to give in to you. Can't even eat in peace.

Jess (*grabbing his wrist*) Thanks, mate.

Stormy Let go.

Jess You'll get it back.

Stormy I will not. Because I won't renege on my principles. No lending money, never have done, never will. I'll give it to you.

Jess You'll do what?

Stormy A present, me to you. (*Finding his pen*) Ask for it and it's yours.

Jess *Ask?*

Stormy Now is that fair or isn't it?

Jess (*getting angry*) Ask you for . . .

Stormy No strings. Ask and ye shall rec . . .

Jess Stick it.

Stormy What?

Jess Stick it where the monkey stuck the . . .

Stormy Hey, now watch your tongue. I'm doing you a good . . .

Jess Well, don't.

Stormy (*waving the cheque book*) Three hundred quid, do you want it or—

Jess walks away, towards where Trina and Myra are sitting

    —don't you? Hey . . .

Trina Myra, you're being silly. Louise would be thrilled. Give it to her.

Jess (*harshly*) Give? Give what?

Myra It's the little medal of the Blessed Virgin. To protect her. (*To Trina*) Jan and Stormy don't believe the way we do.

Trina What odds? It's the thought.

Myra I'd think bad if she took it to humour me.

Trina Louise? Never!

Myra I know full well I'm behind the times. If she made a joke of it . . . (*Deciding*) Ah, no.

Richard It takes so many years and you do so much harm before you own up to it that in your whole life there is you and there are strangers and there is no-one else. There's a clock in the room, and you invite people in for drinks, and hope the chat and the laughing will drown out the noise of it. Well, it doesn't, and after a while you realize they're listening to it, too. You wish they'd go home.

Jan A worse loneliness, is that what you said I was?

Richard Because it nearly worked.

Trina (*to Myra*) If you're all that afraid, let Jan give it to her.

Myra Would she?

Trina Myra, *ask her.*

Myra comes down behind Jan and Richard and stands waiting to interrupt

Jan Nearly is not so bad.

Richard grins and shakes his head

    I'd settle for it.

Richard You would!

Jan's voice is falsely brisk, to disguise an underlying desperation

Jan I'm not going to let you throw our six years away. Tomorrow I'll tell Liz Geraghty it's on again and get the key of her flat.

Richard Don't do that.

Jan Perhaps you'd prefer it if I took another man there and made love to him in our bed? I thought of it. (*With a change of tone*) No-one will find out. We've been careful up to now, we'll be careful in . . .

Trina Myra?

Jan and Richard look around to see Myra staring at them

Richard (*trying to sound casual*) Jan was just saying, she . . .

Myra (*her voice hoarse*) God—forgive—you.

Trina What is it?

The others look around. Myra is too distraught either to realize or care that they are listening

Myra I never believed. I heard in town. I said to people. "If you repeat these lies, that slander . . ."

Stormy What's she on about?

Myra And, oh Jesus, it's true, it's true. As bad as the rest of them, as bad as the worst of them.

Jess (*alarmed, realizing*) Myra . . .

Myra Him that I thought—thought the world of . . . Like—animals.

Richard We were talking . . .

Myra Liar—you liar.

Jess (*going to her*) Will you shut up?

Myra Carrying on these six years—him and her—I heard them.

Jess You misheard.

Richard Sure. All Jan and I were . . .

Myra In front of their own children. No shame in them. The worst—the worst sin. Deny it. To my face, deny that you're dirt. Deny it!

Jan Seeing as it's true, I'm not going to deny anything.

Pause

Richard She . . .

Stormy Seeing as it's what?

Jan As it's true.

Stormy (*violently*) Christ, woman, don't make a joke of it. You can tell she's upset. They were skylarking, Myra, same as we all do.

Jan Terry, what she said about Richard and . . .

Stormy Myra takes things to heart. She's not like us, don't jeer at her.

Jan I'm not . . .

Stormy That'll do!

A moment's pause

Trina (*laughing*) Myra . . . honestly!

Myra stares at her, then at Jan. She finds the religious medal still in her hand and throws it at Jan

Myra Pros—prostitute!

Stormy Ah, now . . .

Jess (*grabbing Myra*) Will you shut your bloody stupid mouth? Will you?

Myra begins to cry

Trina Jess, no. Myra, you made a mistake.

Lou Of course you did.

Myra shakes her head. Trina puts her arm around her

Michael (*after a pause*) What brought *that* on?

Jess (*forcing a grin*) If you think that was something, wait till you see her at the wedding. (*To Richard*) Sorry, mate.

Richard makes a gesture: "Forget it"

Stormy I blame that wine we had. If you've no head for drink . . .
Richard Treacherous.
Stormy (*to Jan*) You all right?
Jan Fine. Just a mistake.
Jess I was on the beach once at the White Rock. Heard one woman saying to another: "I've got a bigger pair than you have. Here—weigh them in your hands." I near broke me neck whipping me head around. They were eating pears.
Stormy That's how it happens.
Jan Jess . . . (*Handing him the medal*) It's Myra's.
Stormy And I'll murder you for making it worse. Sneering at her.
Jan Sorry.
Michael (*with his hand extended*) Hey!
Richard What?
Michael Spot of rain.
Trina I felt it.
Stormy (*looking at the sky*) It'll clear.
Michael I dunno.
Jan So shall we have our coffee or make a beeline?
Trina (*making a face towards Myra*) I could do with a cup.
Stormy And me.
Trina Jan, have you a Thermos?
Jan Mm-hm. (*Going to help*) How is she?
Trina Leave her. (*With compassion for Jan*) Oh, love.
Jan It's *all* right.
Lou (*to Jan*) Hiya, sexy.
Jan You horror.

Jan and Trina set about pouring coffee. Stormy lights a cigarette, Jess sits beside Myra

Jess I never knew you were musical.
Myra (*stubbornly*) I know what I saw.
Jess What you thought you saw.
Myra You took their part.
Jess Maybe you've forgotten what name you called her. You went bonkers.

Myra looks ahead sullenly

Myra, I've got enough troubles, there's vultures in our front garden. At least leave me my friends.
Myra Nice friends!
Jess First thing tomorrow you'll ring up Jan——

Myra Ring up?

Jess —and apologize.

Myra Not to my dying day.

Jess You may be talking of the immediate future. What's it to you what other people get up to? Are you their keeper?

Myra (*tearfully*) Go away.

Jess I'm asking you—why?

Myra (*looking towards Richard*) When—when you have a—high regard for people, and they . . .

Jess (*understanding*) Sure—okay. Poor old Myra; the day you get to heaven there'll be a mass migration.

Stormy comes over to Richard and offers him a cigarette

Stormy Bloody funny world.

Richard Isn't it!

Stormy (*offering a light*) Did yourself and Jan make it up?

Richard freezes and stares at him

You've been giving us the go-by lately. She was peeved.

Richard Pressure of business.

Stormy If that's all it was . . .

Richard What else?

Stormy Good. It takes years to get used to people: be a pity to bugger it up. The time I was starting out in the trade, if a carpenter skimped the job I'd sack him there and then. Every house a model home. Then I got sense. Like with people—you learn to give an inch, put up with what you'd have killed a fellow for ten years ago. The main thing is to stick close. You're in the boat, so stay in it? Yeah?

Richard Right.

Jess comes and stands between them, an arm over each shoulder

Jess You are a pair of thieves, you know that? So when's the next outing?

Stormy Next Sunday?

Richard Why not, while the weather lasts. But this place has had it.

Stormy Can't we move further out: what else are wheels for? If Jemser here is still breathing.

Jess If I'm not, I'll ignore the fact. Good lads—we shall rise again.

Jan Coffee's ready.

Stormy But we'll have a jar Wednesday, what?

They go to collect their coffee. Trina is pressing some on Myra, who shakes her head

Trina Yes, you will: it's good for you. (*She gives both cups to Jess*)

Lou gives coffee to Michael, and they resume an argument, heated

Michael . . . Come on, you can't say that jazz music sprang out of rag-time. Different entities.

Lou One came first, didn't it? Joplin, Marshall, James Scott . . .

Michael So where's the connection with Ellington, Basie, Henderson? Sure, they have Afro-American roots in common, but what else?

Lou It's obvious.

Michael Not to me.

Lou Well, hard luck!

Stormy (*amused*) Hit him, why don't you?

Lou It turns out we're jazz buffs.

Michael You aren't, if you confuse rags and cakewalks with . . .

Stormy Jazz went out years ago.

Michael No, it . . .

Jan It's come in again, darling. The past is fashionable.

Stormy You're coddin'.

Jan It's the in thing.

Richard Any decade but this one.

Stormy (*to Lou and Michael*) Well, God pity the pair of yous. No culture of your own—got to live in Methuselah's time.

Michael Jazz is not archaic, it's . . .

Stormy Go 'long out of that. Why can't yous be up to date? God, we're old fogies, but we know what time we're living in. Where's me player? (*He heads for the cassette player and picks a cassette from the case*)

Jan (*laughing*) I knew it. He'll inflict that thing on us if it kills him.

Stormy Got it. Now come into the present day and listen to this. A bit of shush.

Stormy switches the player on. They listen. We hear McIntyre's "Sentimental Journey"

Michael He's kidding.

Lou It's too much.

Stormy (*beaming*) What? What?

Jan (*laughing*) Oh, really.

Trina, however, smiles and begins to hum to the music

Stormy Isn't that fantastic? "To renew old memories—heaven . . ." Here, Jan—come on, we'll show them. (*He pulls her to him*)

Jan Show them what? Terry, no—I don't w . . . (*Smelling his breath*) You wretch, you've been eating that garlic bread. Get away—ugh!

Stormy Be particular! Trina, then—come here to me: a bit of the Fred and Ginger.

Trina is eager to dance. She looks at Richard

Richard I don't mind.

Trina (*softly, almost affectionately*) And I don't care. I haven't cared this long while. (*She goes to Stormy*)

Stormy (*to the young couple*) Now watch the feet, watch the feet!

Stormy and Trina dance: she with finesse, he making up for his lack of expertise by his enthusiasm. But it is dancing from the jitterbug age. They swing apart, twist, come together

Michael I can't look.
Lou (*laughing; weakly*) Don't m-mock!
Stormy (*to Richard*) Hey, don't leave it to us. (*Motioning*) Jess, get up!

Jan stands in front of Richard

Jan Well, they say if you can't beat them . . .
Richard Garlic bread.

Jan implores him with a look. Richard gets to his feet. Myra looks at him, unforgiving

Stormy There he goes—good lad! Now, Jess . . .
Jess (*to Myra*) It'll make peace.
Myra I will not.
Jess (*between his teeth*) You're going to. (*He forces her to her feet*)
Myra Don't—don't make me.
Jess I say you will.
Stormy Myra, me sound woman.
Jess (*as a comic patter*) I take my wife everywhere I go. It saves kissing her good-bye.
Stormy } Bah-boom! (*Speaking together*)
Jess }
Myra (*to Jess*) No . . .

Jess forces her to dance. He is a terrible dancer, and she is unwilling; they slouch along leadenly. Jan, uncaring, dances close to Richard, her arm about his neck. Michael and Lou watch, choking back their amusement

Stormy Swing it—attagirl. What about that then!

Stormy and Trina lilt to the tune. The music increases in volume. Lou and Michael clap their hands in rhythm. The Lights fade to a Black-out, as—

the CURTAIN *falls*

FURNITURE AND PROPERTY LIST

ACT I

On stage: Celtic cross
Effect of trees
Wooden picnic table. *On it:* remains of a picnic for 8 people—used plates, glasses, food, bottles of wine, napkins, cutlery, cellophane bags, etc. *Beside it:* hamper
2 benches
2 folding stools
Sunday Times (for **Richard**)

Off stage: Book—*Shell Guide to Ireland* **(Lou)**
Car keys **(Lou)**

Personal: **Jess:** packet of cigarettes, lighter, watch, bank notes, pencil, dirty handkerchief
Michael: guitar
Trina: mirror in handbag
Jan: watch
Stormy: 2 crumpled pound notes

ACT II

Strike: Celtic cross
Trees
Any remains from picnic

Set: Notice board
Part of crane or mechanical digger

Off stage: Picnic hamper **(Stormy)**
Picnic hamper **(Michael)**
Freezer bag **(Trina)**
Papier-mâché attaché case **(Myra)**
Divided among the above containers are items for the picnic, including: chicken, ham, potato salad, sandwiches, French bread, garlic bread, cheese, pickles, strawberries, bottles of wine, Thermos of coffee, plates, cutlery, corkscrew, mugs, etc.
Rug **(Stormy)**
Cassette player with tape of Beatles number **(Stormy)**
Spare cassette tape with McIntyre number **(Stormy)**
2 stools **(Richard)**
Rug, cushion **(Trina)**

Personal: **Lou:** sunglasses
Myra: medal on chain
Stormy: nest of metal cups, full hip-flask, cigarettes, lighter, cheque book, pen
Jess: grubby handkerchief

LIGHTING PLOT

Property fittings required: nil
Exterior. A hillside. The same scene throughout

ACT I   Day

To open: General effect of hot sunshine
Cue 1   **Jan:** "Now please." **Michael** strums guitar   (Page 14)
             Lighting changes to spots on separated couples
Cue 2   **Jess:** ". . . get the new suit." Guitar chord   (Page 16)
             Revert to previous lighting
Cue 3   **Lou** and **Michael** exit   (Page 21)
             Lighting change to indicate lapse of hours—towards sunset
Cue 4   **Lou** and **Michael** exit   (Page 33)
             Bring up blinding white light over whole stage, followed
               by Black-out

ACT II   Day

To open: General effect of rather hard, chilly sunlight
Cue 5   *As whole Cast dance and* CURTAIN *falls*   (Page 59)
             Fade to Black-out

EFFECTS PLOT

ACT I

Cue 1   **Jan:** "You'd run ten miles."   (Page 23)
             Church bell rings for one minute

ACT II

No cues

MADE AND PRINTED IN GREAT BRITAIN BY
LATIMER TREND & COMPANY LTD PLYMOUTH
MADE IN ENGLAND